GW00703156

The Apple TV
PocketGuide

Second Edition

Jeff**Carlson**

All the Secrets of the Apple TV, Pocket Sized.

**Peachpit
Press**

The Apple TV Pocket Guide, Second Edition
Jeff Carlson

Peachpit Press
1249 Eighth Street
Berkeley, CA 94710
510/524-2178
510/524-2221 (fax)

Find us on the Web at: www.peachpit.com
To report errors, please send a note to errata@peachpit.com

Peachpit Press is a division of Pearson Education

Editor: Clifford Colby
Copyeditor: Liane Thomas
Production editor: Lisa Brazieal
Compositor: Jeff Carlson
Indexer: Rebecca Plunkett
Cover design: Aren Howell
Cover photography: Jeff Carlson
Interior design: Kim Scott, with Maureen Forys

ISBN-13: 978-0-321-56315-6
ISBN-10:   0-321-56315-8

9 8 7 6 5 4 3 2 1

Printed and bound in the United States of America

For Jill, Steve, Aidan, and Lina

Acknowledgments

You probably have an image in your head of a book writer: holed up in an attic office space, alone, sleep-deprived, heading downstairs occasionally for coffee and sugar and the stray bit of protein. Well, yeah, that's pretty much true. However, I wasn't alone. Well, physically alone maybe, but always connected to a fantastic group of people who helped make it possible and who have my thanks.

First and foremost, Agen G. N. Schmitz stepped in to help update the content while I was becoming a dad for the first time. If it weren't for him, you wouldn't be seeing this book for months, I'm sure.

At Apple, Teresa Brewer, Keri Walker, Jennifer Hakes, Janette Barrios, and Jai Chulani provided me with equipment and answers when I needed them for both editions of this book.

At Sony, Greg Belloni and Aaron Levine loaned me a beautiful Sony 40-inch Bravia widescreen LCD television so I could get the full effect of playing HD video from the Apple TV. Want it.

Liane Thomas provided her usual high degree of sharp-eyed copyediting. Rebecca Plunkett shouldered the unenviable task of producing the index on a tight deadline.

My editors and production editor at Peachpit Press once again applied the right combination of hand-holding and whip-cracking: Cliff Colby, Lisa Brazieal, and Nancy Davis.

I also want to thank my officemates Kim Ricketts, Weston Clay, and Glenn Fleishman, who shared his wireless networking knowledge. I referred often to his book *Take Control of Your 802.11n AirPort Extreme Network* (www.takecontrolbooks.com).

Most deserving of thanks is my wife, Kimberly, who endured my work schedule while encouraging me the entire time, and Eliana, who didn't know what Dad was doing but liked the colors on the screen.

About Jeff Carlson

Jeff Carlson gave up an opportunity to intern at a design firm during college because he suspected they really just wanted someone tall to play on their volleyball team. In the intervening years, he's been a designer and writer, authoring best-selling books on the Macintosh, Web design, video editing, digital photography, and Palm organizers. He's currently a columnist for the *Seattle Times*, the Managing Editor of the respected electronic newsletter *TidBITS* (www.tidbits.com), and consumes almost too much coffee. Almost. Find me at jeffcarlson.com and neverenoughcoffee.com.

Contents

Meet the Apple TV .... **xiii**

Chapter 1: Get Hooked Up **1**

Connect the TV and Stereo............................... 2
  HDMI 2
  HDMI to DVI *4*
  Component video....................................... 4
  Analog audio 5
  Optical audio 5

Power On 6

Chapter 2: Connect to Your Network **9**

Networking Overview................................... 10
  Typical Ethernet...................................... 10
  Typical wireless 11
  Single-computer wireless.............................. 11

Connect to the Network 12
  Ethernet setup.. 13
  Wireless setup.. 14

Configure TCP/IP 16
  DHCP... 16
  Manual IP 17

Download Updates...................................... 19
  How to Get the Version 2.0 Update..................... 19

Set Up the First Sync................................... 20

Chapter 3: Interface and Navigation. 23

The Apple TV Interface 24
  The Apple Remote 24
    Pair the remote 27
    Unpair the remote 28
    Lost the remote? 29

General Settings 30
  About 30
    About the device 30
    Network 31
  iTunes Store 31
  Update Software 31
  Language 31
  Legal 31
  Reset Settings 32

The Screen Saver 32
  Settings 32
    Timeout 33
    Use for Music 33
    Preview 33
    Albums 34
    Photos 35
    Slideshow 35

Video Settings 36
    Closed Captioning 36
    TV Resolution 36
    HDMI Output 36

Chapter 4: Buy and Rent Media 37

Enter the iTunes Store 38
  Browse for content 39
  Search for content 40
  Power Search 42

Buy from iTunes 42
   Set up an iTunes account 43
   Buy now..44
   Shopping cart 44

Get a TV Show Season Pass 44
   Get a TV Show Multi-Pass............................45

Rent Movies Using iTunes 47
   Transfer Rented Movies to the Apple TV 48

Buy and Rent Media Using the Apple TV 49
   Browse for Content 50
   Search for Content...................................50
   Buy or Rent..51
   Movies *52*
   TV Shows *53*
   Music..*55*

Chapter 5: Watch Movies,
            TV Shows, and YouTube 57

Screen a Movie... 58
   Watch movie trailers.................................58
   Choose a movie...................................... 60
   Choose a purchased movie...........................*60*
   Choose a rented movie *61*
   Watch a movie..63
   Pause and resume *63*
   Jump back or jump ahead *64*
   Skip in 10-second increments *64*
   Fast-forward or rewind *65*
   Slow motion..*66*

Watch a TV Show.. 66
   Show view 67
   Date view 68

Closed Captioning..................................... 70

Watch YouTube Videos 71
  Log In to Your Account 71
  Find and Play YouTube Videos 72
  History 74
  Search 74

Parental Controls 75
  Permissions *77*
  Ratings *78*

**Chapter 6: Play Music, Podcasts,
            and Audiobooks** **79**

Play Music 80
  Choose a song 80
  Shuffle Songs *80*
  Music Videos *81*
  Playlists *81*
  Artists *82*
  Albums *82*
  Songs *82*
  Genres *83*
  Composers *83*
  Audiobooks *83*
  Scrolling 83
  Play a song 84
  Now Playing *86*
  Audio settings 87
  Repeat Music *87*
  Sound Check *87*
  Sound Effects *88*
  Dolby Digital Out *88*
  AirTunes *88*

Set Up iTunes Playlists 90
  Playlist 90

Create a playlist based on selection *91*
Rearrange items in a playlist *92*
Smart Playlist...**92**
Editing and deleting playlists *95*

Podcasts **98**
Podcasts on the Apple TV **99**
Favorites *101*
Search for podcasts *101*
Podcasts from iTunes **101**
From the iTunes Store *102*
From an RSS link...*103*
Unsubscribe from a podcast *104*
Podcast settings **104**

Audiobooks **106**

Chapter 7: View Photo Slideshows **107**

Sync and Stream Photos **108**
Photo sources...**108**
Sync photos to the Apple TV **109**
Stream photos from another computer **111**

Play a Slideshow **112**
Slideshow settings.................................... **113**
Time Per Slide *113*
Music..*113*
Repeat...*114*
Shuffle Photos *114*
Shuffle Music...*114*
Ken Burns Effect...*114*
Transitions *115*

Create Better Slideshows **116**
Use Smart Photo Albums **116**
iPhoto...*117*

Aperture. 118
Photoshop Elements. 118
Create a Custom Slideshow 119
iPhoto. 120
Output as Movie. 121

View Online Photos 123
Flickr 123
Add a contact 123
Viewing photos. 124
Add your contacts' contacts. 125
.Mac Web Gallery 126
Specify a gallery location 126

Chapter 8: Sync and Stream. 129

Sync Media Between the Computer and Apple TV 130
Too much media. 130
Authorization 131
Automatic Sync in iTunes. 133
Custom Sync in iTunes. 134
Movies 135
TV shows 136
Music. 136
Podcasts. 137
Photos. 138
Sync between Apple TV and an iPod 138
Change the sync source. 140
Sync one computer with multiple Apple TVs 141
Remove a synced Apple TV 142

Stream Media from Other Computers 143
Set up streaming 145
Streamed versus synced playback. 148
Remove a streaming source. 149
Use streaming sources only. 150

Chapter 9: Prepare Movies for Apple TV 151

Ripping DVDs 152
   Convert DVD content 153
   Encode with HandBrake (Mac) *155*
   Encode with DVD to Apple TV Converter (Windows) *156*
   Add the movie to iTunes *158*
   Rip television episodes from DVD 158
   Encoding settings, explained 159
   Codec *160*
   Bitrate *160*
   Resolution *161*
   Framerate *161*
   File format *162*

Convert HD Content 162

Convert Your Own Movies 164
   Export the video 164
   iMovie '08 . . . . *164*
   Windows Movie Maker *165*

Add Metadata 167
   Set a preview icon 168

Chapter 10: Troubleshooting .171

First Steps 172

Network Issues 172

Apple Remote Not Working 173

Restart the Apple TV 174

Enter Diagnostic Mode 175

Restore Factory Settings 175

Index 177

Meet the Apple TV

Very few people sit down with a bowl of popcorn and expect a pleasant evening in front of the *computer*. Although you can watch movies and television shows on your Mac or PC, the experience is shackled by tradeoffs: Computer monitors are designed for viewing at close range, not across the room; you must navigate the computer's operating system; the computer is likely not in the living room.

And yet, more entertainment is coming into our homes via computers and the Internet. The Apple TV is the bridge between your computer and television, making it easy for you to watch digital content from the comfort of your couch, not your office chair.

What It Does

If you're like many people, you probably have a set-top box connected to your television that brings in cable or satellite TV signals. The Apple TV is a similar device, but it delivers video, music, and photos from the Internet and one or more computers on your home network.

Thanks to the Apple TV's hard drive, you can copy and store media from one computer, just like connecting an iPod. By *synchronizing* media in this way, you can play back content even if the computer is powered off or not connected to the network.

If your household includes more than one computer, you can *stream* content to the Apple TV without copying it to the hard drive first. The benefit is being able to watch material from any computer without first having to copy the content to the Apple TV.

Version 2.0 of the Apple TV software, released in February 2008, added the capability to rent movies— including high-definition movies—and purchase movies, TV shows, and music directly on the Apple TV.

What it doesn't do

When the Apple TV was first announced, many people (myself included) were disappointed that it didn't offer the single greatest television feature in the world: time-shifting. In other words, the Apple TV is not a TiVo, recording broadcast television programs for playback whenever it's convenient (and skipping past commercials).

When you think about it, however, this is not surprising at all: Apple sells TV shows and movies through the iTunes Store, so offering the capability to record broadcast TV would undercut the iTunes business (and lessen the likelihood that entertainment studios would make their shows available on iTunes).

The Apple TV is also not a DVD player, though you can rip DVDs you own for disc-free playback (see Chapter 9 for instructions on how to convert movies to a format that the Apple TV—and iPods—can play).

The good news is, the Apple TV doesn't *need* to deal with DVDs or live television programming. It can exist with other components that handle those functions (see Chapter 1).

Does Apple TV Replace the AirPort Express?

Apple sells another streaming media box, the AirPort Express, which connects to a stereo system and streams music from iTunes running on a computer on your network. The advantage of the Apple TV is that you can navigate your music collection on your television screen, rather than dashing over to the computer hosting the music.

The AirPort Express has its own advantages. It can act as a wireless base station, providing Internet access to other computers on the network; you can simultaneously stream music to several AirPort Express devices; and it can be a network print server, letting you print to a USB printer from any computer in the house. But for just streaming media, the Apple TV is the better performer.

What You Need

If you're skimming this book in an Apple Store or
other retail location, waiting for someone to fetch an
Apple TV from the stock in the back, make sure you
go home with the right gear. If you're already home,
check the following list to see if you need to make
a quick run to pick up something. Because once the
Apple TV is hooked up and running, believe me, you
won't want to leave the couch for hours.

- **APPLE TV.** You won't get far without one of these.

- **WIDESCREEN HIGH-DEFINITION OR "ENHANCED
  DEFINITION" TELEVISION.** Sorry, the 10-year-old box
  you brought from college just won't cut it. The TV
  needs to support widescreen (a 16:9 aspect ratio)
  resolutions of 1080i, 720p, 576p, or 480p, and
  include HDMI, DVI, or component ports.

If you've purchased a standard-definition television
within the last couple of years, check its connections
on the back. It may include component video and audio
ports, in which case the Apple TV will work. However, if
you're in the market to buy a new TV, skip these models
and get an HDTV; the quality and widescreen aspect
ratio going forward will be worth whatever money you
would have saved with the standard-definition model.

- **HDMI OR COMPONENT VIDEO AND AUDIO CABLES.**
  The Apple TV doesn't include cables, so make
  sure you buy the type that connect to your TV.
  Note that component cables are not the same as
  composite cables. See Chapter 1 for more detail.

tip Beware of cable prices! If someone is asking for much more than $20 for an HDMI or component cable, go elsewhere. The Apple Store sells XtremeMac cables for $20, and you can find others online for less.

- **COMPUTER.** The Apple TV gets its content from a Mac or Windows-based PC.

- **ITUNES.** If you don't already have it, download iTunes at www.apple.com/itunes/.

- **LOCAL NETWORK.** Media is transferred over wired Ethernet or wireless network (see Chapter 1).

HDTV Resolutions Explained

The "i" and "p" in video resolutions refer to the two ways video is drawn to the screen. Most regular televisions are *interlaced*, meaning that every other horizontal line is drawn in one pass (lines 1, 3, 5, and so on), followed by the alternating lines in the next pass (lines 2, 4, 6, and so on). This process happens quickly, so our eyes view both passes as one solid image. The other method is *progressive*, where each frame of video is drawn in its entirety.

The number represents how many horizontal lines are drawn (also known as *vertical resolution*). So, those resolution specs break down like this:

- **1080i:** 1,920 by 1080 pixels, interlaced

- **720p:** 1,280 by 720 pixels, progressive

- **576p:** 720 by 576 pixels, progressive

- **480p:** 720 by 480 pixels, progressive

(The horizontal resolution figure can vary, depending on the television model, which is why the terms are defined by their vertical resolution.)

1

Get Hooked Up

If you've ever gotten trapped in a snake's nest of cables behind the TV, you know that making several video and audio components work together isn't easy. Starting out from scratch, it can be a no-sweat operation. But more than likely you'll be attempting to Borg together the Apple TV with other equipment.

The upside is that Apple has intentionally limited your choices. The Apple TV contains only a few ports for connecting to your television and stereo, which cuts down the number of cables while still delivering all that color and stereo sound. Grab a flashlight, make room behind the TV, and let's get started.

Connect the TV and Stereo

Generally speaking, follow these steps to hook up the Apple TV:

1. Connect the Apple TV and the television using either HDMI or component video cables.

2. If you're outputting audio to a device other than the television, connect the Apple TV using analog or optical audio cables.

3. Plug in the Apple TV's power cable.

 tip The Apple TV does not include an on/off switch, so connecting the power cable turns it on. The device checks for available video and audio equipment at launch, so make sure your other cables are connected before you plug in the power cable.

HDMI

Figure 1.1
HDMI cable.

If you've not yet run across devices with HDMI (High-Definition Multimedia Interface) connections, you soon will. HDMI can deliver video and audio over one cable, making setup a breeze (**Figure 1.1**). But more important, HDMI can push digital video formats ranging from standard-definition (SD) to uncompressed high-definition (HD) variants, meaning this standard should be around for a while (also see the sidebar at right).

Connect the cable to the HDMI port on the back of the Apple TV (**Figure 1.2**), and plug the other end into the HDMI port on your television. Done!

Figure 1.2
If you're connecting using an HDMI cable, your work here is almost finished.

 tip What if your TV's HDMI port is already being used by another device? Get an inexpensive HDMI switcher that lets you plug in more than one HDMI cable.

HDCP

Another reason we're likely to see HDMI for a while is HDCP, or High-bandwidth Digital Content Protection (no, I don't know why they left the B out of the acronym, either). HDCP is, unfortunately, a potential poison pill for HDMI. It's a digital rights management (DRM) system meant to ensure that only properly licensed content can be played over an HDMI cable. So, if you were nefarious and tried to play a bootleg DVD, and your DVD player connected to your television, HDCP could kick in and simply not play the movie on the TV. Or, more importantly, if your device didn't properly recognize the HDCP, your legal content may still not play.

Some movies that Apple sells or rents are protected by HDCP, a fact I ran into recently when I tried to play a rented movie on a screen with no HDMI port—I had an HDMI-to-DVI cable providing the video connection. Without HDMI and HDCP, I couldn't watch the movie. However, HDCP doesn't apply over component connections, so the movie played fine in that configuration (see the next page).

HDMI to DVI

Although HDMI is quickly becoming the standard for widescreen TVs, some sets use DVI, the same type of connector on many computer displays. In fact, a friend of mine recently bought a 20-inch Dell monitor to use as a TV instead of a more expensive HDTV (but see the sidebar on the previous page).

You can buy an HDMI-to-DVI cable (or just an adapter if you already have a cable with HDMI at both ends). The only catch is that DVI doesn't carry audio, so you'd need to connect an analog or optical audio cable to hear the sound.

note Notice that the Apple TV offers only one of each type of video port. It doesn't support pass-through of signals to other devices, the way some VCRs do.

Component video

Figure 1.3
Component
video cable.

The other video option is to connect a component cable between the Apple TV and your television (**Figure 1.3**). Three plugs carry the red, green, and blue video signals that make up the image you see.

Unlike HDMI, component cables carry only video, which means you'll need to connect audio cables from the Apple TV to your television or stereo (unless you want to relive those silent movie days—music videos, especially, are fun to watch without sound).

note Don't confuse component with *composite* video, which uses one connector for video (labeled in yellow) and two connectors for audio (red and white).

note When both video types are connected, HDMI overrides component video and audio.

Analog audio

Figure 1.4
Analog
audio cable.

To get sound out of the Apple TV (if you're not using HDMI), you'll need an audio cable. The most common is analog audio, which features two plugs on each end, one red and one white, corresponding to the left and right audio channels (**Figure 1.4**).

Connect the cable to the red and white audio ports on the Apple TV (**Figure 1.5**), and to the corresponding ports on your television or on your stereo receiver.

Figure 1.5
Component
video and
composite
audio cables
connected.

Optical audio

Figure 1.6
Optical audio.

The other audio option is to plug a Toslink fiber-optic cable to the optical audio port on the back of the Apple TV (**Figure 1.6**) if your television or stereo supports optical connections.

Optical audio is entirely digital, so in theory an optical connection will produce higher-quality sound (though of course that's also dependent on your other gear).

Power On

With the video and audio connected, it's time to power up the Apple TV. Make sure the television is set to the correct input (check the instructions that came with the TV), and insert the power cable (**Figure 1.7**). The LED on the front of the box blinks yellow, and an Apple logo appears on your screen.

note

Want to see a tiny example of Apple's smart industrial design? The end of the power plug is gray except for the portion that gets inserted into the device, which is white. When the white disappears, you know the plug is securely connected.

Figure 1.7
Plugging in the power cable starts up the Apple TV.

When you power up, the Apple TV attempts to determine the best video mode, so don't be surprised if the screen flickers as it tries various resolutions. Some televisions display the current setting in a corner of the screen.

note If you don't see anything at all, and the light on the front of the Apple TV is on, check your TV's input source and that all of the cables are fastened tight. If that does nothing, grab the remote that came with the Apple TV. Press and hold the Menu and Menu up/scroll (+) buttons for several seconds. The device will cycle through its list of resolutions; when the message "If you can see the Apple logo, select OK" appears, press the Select/Play/Pause button (the center one) on the remote.

After a few seconds, the light on the front of the device becomes solid white.

Next, you're asked to choose a language (**Figure 1.8**).

1. Using the included remote, press the Menu up/scroll (+) and Menu down/scroll (−) buttons to highlight a language.

2. Press the Select/Play/Pause button in the middle of the button ring to make your selection.

Figure 1.8
Choose your preferred language.

You're in! Time to connect to your home network.

In this chapter, we've covered every port on the back of the Apple TV except two: the Ethernet port, discussed in the next chapter, offers a wired connection to your home network; and the USB port, which...does nothing. At least, that's what Apple wants you to believe. Its true purpose is to allow Apple to perform diagnostics and servicing, and is therefore not for your use. That hasn't stopped some enterprising hackers from trying (and succeeding) to enable the port. However, doing so isn't easy to do, will void your warranty, and is beyond the scope of this book. If you're curious, poke around at www.appletvhacks.net.

Where's the Off Switch?

There isn't one. Although the Apple TV is really a Mac OS X computer at heart, there's no way to shut it down the way you would a computer, aside from pulling the plug (which probably isn't a good idea to do regularly).

However, you can put it into standby mode if you want. Simply hold the Select/Play/Pause button for 6–10 seconds. The screen goes black, audio stops playing, and the hard drive spins down. This doesn't put it completely to sleep, however. It still responds to network connections and appears in the iTunes library of the computer to which it's synced. Also, if it was syncing content when put into standby mode, the synchronization will continue (for more on syncing, see Chapter 8).

To wake it from standby mode, press any button on the remote.

2

Connect to Your Network

A DVD player plays back movies from the discs you insert into it. Your TV set-top box gets broadcast programming from a cable strung to your house or a satellite dish mounted on the roof.

The Apple TV gets its content from the computers on your home network, or directly from the iTunes Store. The Ethernet port connects to traditional wired networks, but unless you've strung cables through the house (which often involves drilling holes in walls and floors), you probably want to take advantage of the Apple TV's built-in wireless networking.

Networking Overview

A network can comprise millions of computers, but for our purposes, here are a few common setups that are likely to match what you have in your home. What's important is that the Apple TV can connect to the Internet; being able to connect to at least one computer is also beneficial. (Version 2.0 of the Apple TV software enables direct downloads; the original incarnation required synchronizing to a computer.)

Typical Ethernet

Figure 2.1
Ethernet cable.

Your Internet connection comes into the house via a broadband modem (either cable or DSL) that you or your Internet service provider (ISP) set up. The modem is connected to your computer via an Ethernet cable (**Figure 2.1**).

Some broadband modems also have extra Ethernet ports to connect more computers via Ethernet. If that's not the case, you probably have an Ethernet switch or hub between the modem and the computer to connect other computers.

To connect the Apple TV, run a cable from the modem or switch to its Ethernet port (**Figure 2.2**).

Figure 2.2
A common Ethernet network setup.

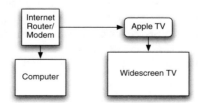

Typical wireless

As in the previous example, the Internet connection comes into the house via a modem; some ISPs provide models that also act as wireless routers. More commonly, however, an additional wireless router (also sometimes called a base station) connects to the broadband modem via Ethernet. Apple's AirPort Extreme Base Station is an example.

The wireless router transmits data to and from one or more computers over the air and acts as a traffic cop between machines.

In this setup, the Apple TV operates as just another computer on the network, using its built-in wireless capability to transfer data to and from the base station (**FIGURE 2.3**).

Figure 2.3
A typical wireless network setup.

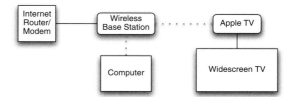

Single-computer wireless

If you own just one computer, you don't necessarily need to buy a wireless router to network the Apple TV. As long as your computer has wireless capabilities, you can set it up to act as the base station. To learn how to set up this unusual configuration, go to jeffcarlson.com/appletv/single_wireless.html.

The Wireless Alphabet

"Wireless networking" is a broad term that encompasses a number of networking protocols, such as 802.11b. The "802.11" is the name of the IEEE (Institute of Electrical and Electronics Engineers) working group that determines wireless networking standards, and the following letter refers to a specific version. The Apple TV supports the main protocols in use:

- **802.11b** operates at a theoretical maximum of 11 Mbps (megabits-per-second), with a real-world speed of 5.5 Mbps.

- **802.11g** operates at 54 Mbps (you may see products sometimes advertised as "54g"), with a real-world speed of 25 Mbps.

- **802.11n** is the latest version, running at a maximum of 300 Mbps, with real-world speeds of 100 Mbps. However, the 802.11n specification isn't going to be final until late 2008. Because it takes so long to finalize a standard, companies have been shipping "Draft N" equipment, which *should* work together but could run into glitches. If you're using an Apple AirPort Extreme Base Station and a recent N-compatible Mac, of course, it should all just work. If you have a wireless base station from another company, it's possible you might experience some incompatibilities. When the final spec is released, however, expect to see the equipment manufacturers release firmware updates that bring the hardware in line.

Connect to the Network

After you choose a language at the first startup, the Apple TV immediately looks for a network connection. To avoid confusion, it prioritizes Ethernet over wireless networking. If an Ethernet cable is attached and the network is active, Ethernet is used. If not, the Apple TV searches for an available wireless network.

Since we're setting up the Apple TV for the first time, I'm listing steps as you would encounter them at startup. However, you can always return to these network configuration screens later by choosing Network in the Settings screen.

Ethernet setup

The most difficult part of using Ethernet may be stringing networking cable through the house— most likely, your Internet router is located in a room far away from the television. (Okay, I'll admit it, I'm a homeowner with an embarrassing lack of do-it-your-self building skills. Wireless networking must have been developed with people like me in mind.)

However, Ethernet offers a couple of advantages: It offers faster data transfer speeds than wireless networking, and it isn't subject to signal interference the way wireless is. You may also have a wired Ethernet network already installed, or perhaps none of your computers are wireless-capable.

 Ethernet is also useful when performing the first synchronization with the Apple TV; see the end of this chapter for more details.

With an Ethernet cable attached, the first message you'll see after choosing a language is "Connecting to the network." What happens next depends on how IP (Internet protocol) addresses are assigned on your network:

- **DHCP.** Your network's router hands out IP addresses automatically.

- **MANUALLY.** Each computer on your network is identified by a specific IP address.

If your network uses DHCP (which is most common, as you'll learn later in this chapter), you're all done. Feel free to skip to Chapter 3. If not, see "Configure TCP/IP," later in this chapter.

 tip   **Even if you've already set up a wireless network, connecting an Ethernet cable switches the Apple TV to the wired network.**

Wireless setup

After a moment of scanning, the Apple TV displays a list of available wireless networks (**FIGURE 2.4**).

Figure 2.4
Apple TV lists nearby wireless networks.

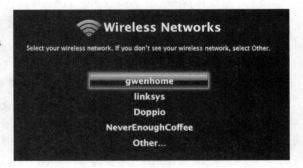

To establish a connection, follow these steps:

1. Use the remote's Menu up/scroll (+) and Menu down/scroll (–) buttons to select the name of your wireless network. (For more on the Apple Remote, see Chapter 3.)

note As an extra precaution, some people choose to create a closed network when they set up their wireless routers, which does not broadcast the network's name. If this is the case for you, choose Other. On the next screen, use the remote to enter the network name and then choose Done.

2. Press the Select/Play/Pause button in the center of the remote to choose that network.

3. If the network is protected using a WEP password, choose the type of password to enter:

   WEP PASSWORD: Human-readable alphanumeric password, such as "dog" (though of course that's a terrible password).

   WEP 40/128-BIT HEX AND WEP 40/128-BIT ASCII: Some base stations use coded passwords in hex or ASCII text; check your router's instructions for more information.

   If your network is protected with the increasingly common and much more secure WPA (Wireless Protected Access) protocol, you'll go directly to the next step.

tip The Apple TV does not support the WPA-Enterprise protocol. You'd need to change your router to provide WPA-Personal instead.

4. On the Wireless Password screen, use the remote to enter the network's password, character by character, and then choose Done (**FIGURE 2.5**, next page). (This screen does not appear if your network is unprotected.)

Figure 2.5
The remote is a
bit tedious for
entering text,
but it works.

 Pressing the Previous/Rewind (left) button at the left
edge of a line moves the cursor to the far right edge, so
you don't have to scroll all the way across the screen.

Configure TCP/IP

After the Apple TV establishes a connection with the
wireless network, it attempts to gain Internet access
using TCP/IP, the system of assigning addresses to all
connected machines. TCP/IP is configured in one of
two ways: DHCP or manual IP.

DHCP

Most home networks use DHCP (Dynamic Host
Control Protocol) to direct traffic between the
Internet and your computers. When a computer (or
in this case, the Apple TV) is added to the network,
the wireless router or modem automatically assigns
an IP address.

DHCP is like checking into a hotel: The clerk tells you which room you're staying in and can send messages to you in that room for the duration of your stay.

If your network uses DHCP, there's no more configuration left to do. The Apple TV's snazzy startup animation plays, and you're asked to associate with a computer running iTunes (feel free to skip ahead to Chapter 3).

Manual IP

Alternatively, your network may use a set of specific IP numbers to identify connected computers. Using the earlier analogy, this would be like living in an apartment that has a fixed, private address.

The Apple TV first attempts to connect using DHCP because that's the most common approach. If that doesn't work, a Connection Failed screen appears (**Figure 2.6**).

Figure 2.6
You'll see this screen if your network needs a manual IP address.

To assign a manual IP address, make sure you have the IP address information (your ISP may have provided this) and do the following:

1. Choose Configure TCP/IP.

2. On the Network setup screen, choose Manually.

3. Enter the IP address to be assigned to the Apple TV. Press the Menu up/scroll (+) and Menu down/scroll (–) buttons to select each number, then press the Next/Fast-Forward button to go to the next number. Choose Done when you're finished.

4. On the next screen, enter the subnet mask in the same manner and choose Done.

5. On the next screen, enter the IP address of your router and choose Done.

6. If you need to enter a DNS server address, do that on the following screen, then choose Done.

7. Lastly, the Apple TV asks you to choose your wireless network again and enter its password. Once that's completed, it establishes the connection.

note A connection to the Internet isn't completely necessary; as shown in the Connection Failed screen, you can choose to continue without an Internet connection. However, doing so will prevent you from playing back protected content purchased from the iTunes Store (the first time, at least; see Chapter 4). You also won't be able to rent movies, view movie trailers, listen to song samples from the iTunes Store, buy music, watch previews of music videos, or have the Apple TV check for software updates.

Download Updates

To check if any software updates are available, do the following:

1. Press the Menu button on the Apple Remote.

2. Scroll to Settings in the left pane of the dual-pane menu using the Menu down/scroll (–) button.

3. Press the Next/Fast-Forward button to move to the right pane and scroll to Downloads, then press the Select/Play/Pause button.

4. On the next screen, press Select/Play/Pause to check for downloads.

 The Apple TV automatically makes periodic checks for updates, and it displays the last time it did so beneath the large icon at the left.

How to Get the Version 2.0 Update

If your Apple TV is still using the version 1.1 software, do the following to upgrade to Apple TV 2.0:

1. In the main menu, scroll down to Settings and press Select/Play/Pause.

2. In the next screen, scroll down to Update Software and press Select/Play/Pause.

3. After the Apple TV finds the update, choose Download Now to get it started, or Update Later if you're not quite ready (**FIGURE 2.7**, next page).

Figure 2.7
Give the
go-ahead to
update to
version 2.0.

Apple TV Update

The Apple TV update has finished downloading. Do you want to install it now?

Your Apple TV will restart to begin installing the update. Do not unplug your Apple TV
while it is updating.

Update Now
Update Later

4. After the update has downloaded, an Update
Now message appears; press Select/Play/Pause
to make it so.

The Apple TV then proceeds to do its installation
dance, which takes several restarts to accomplish.
When the update has finished, you'll see the new
colorful opening video and the menu interface of
Apple TV 2.0 (see Chapter 3).

tip If your Apple TV shipped with the 1.0 or 1.1 software and
you update to version 2.0, restoring it to the factory
default reverts to that original version. You would then
need to download the 2.0 update again. See Chapter 10
for more on resetting the Apple TV.

Set Up the First Sync

Now that the Apple TV is hooked into your home
network, you should see a random five-digit number
in large text (**Figure 2.8**). This is the gateway to
accessing movies and music managed by iTunes on
your computer.

Figure 2.8
This code establishes a relationship with iTunes.

Apple initially assumes you want to *synchronize* the Apple TV, which copies media from your computer to the box's internal hard drive. This is the same behavior as the iPod: you associate it with one computer.

 tip You're not required to sync with a computer—it's just the more common approach, which is why this option appears right after you've set up the Apple TV's network connection for the first time. You could instead stream content, which sends it over the network in real time. I discuss syncing and streaming in more detail in Chapter 8, but for now, if you want to stream instead of sync, press the Menu button to bypass this screen.

To set up the association, do the following:

Figure 2.9
Devices list.

1. On your Mac or PC, launch iTunes. (If you don't have iTunes 7.6 or later installed, download it for free from www.apple.com/itunes/.)

2. Click the Apple TV item that appears in the Devices list in the left-hand column (**Figure 2.9**).

3. Enter the five-digit number on your TV screen
(**Figure 2.10**). iTunes verifies the passcode with
the Apple TV.

4. In the next screen that appears, name your Apple
TV; this step differentiates this device from other
Apple TVs you may own.

Figure 2.10
Enter the same
code in iTunes
that the Apple
TV displays.

Set Up Your tv

Please enter the passcode displayed on your Apple TV to
allow iTunes to sync or stream your media.

9 1 8 1

5. Click OK. The Apple TV contacts the iTunes Store
to verify that the computer is authorized to play
purchased content. When that's done, it starts to
copy media to the hard drive.

Depending on how much media you have and the
type of network you're using, synchronization could
take a while. If you're using an 802.11b or 802.11g
wireless network, consider connecting the Apple TV
via Ethernet for the first sync.

The good news is that you don't have to wait for
the sync to finish before you start enjoying your
media. If you want to watch a movie right away, for
example, it will be streamed over the network. When
the synchronization is finished, Apple TV plays your
content directly from the hard drive.

tip

**When you play movies or TV shows during a sync, the
sync process is paused so that playback can use as much
bandwidth as needed. Syncing will resume when you're
done watching the show.**

3

Interface and Navigation

When first introduced, the Apple TV's navigation system owed a large debt to the enormously popular iPod. However, each step through the menus required loading a new screen.

The user interface of Apple TV's second generation is now a dual-pane menu system that floats over the background selections from the iTunes store (or YouTube videos or your photos). It's not a radical departure, but it enables you to more easily view all your options, from movies, TV shows, and music stored on the Apple TV, to movie rentals available at the iTunes Store.

The Apple TV Interface

The main menu is split into two panes, with top-level media types and Apple TV settings listed on the left. Secondary choices on the right change based on the selection in the first pane (**Figure 3.1**).

Figure 3.1
The main screen.

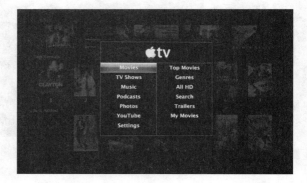

A glossy, two-tone blue rectangle indicates which item is selected in either pane, with the main heading of a section dimmed on the left when you're navigating the submenu options on the right.

The Apple Remote

The Apple Remote is quite a change from the heavily studded, multi-button remotes that come with most every other audio or video device (**Figure 3.2**). Instead of offering a button for every feature, its six buttons move you through the Apple TV interface, which controls every feature.

Figure 3.2
Who stole all
the buttons?

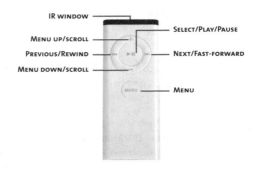

IR WINDOW

MENU UP/SCROLL

PREVIOUS/REWIND

MENU DOWN/SCROLL

SELECT/PLAY/PAUSE

NEXT/FAST-FORWARD

MENU

You've probably picked this up by now, but here's
how the remote works:

• Press Menu up/scroll (+) and Menu down/scroll
  (–) to move the selection up or down in the list.

• Press Select/Play/Pause to choose the item that's
  selected. In the dual-pane menu, doing so on
  the left switches the active blue rectangle to the
  right, where you can select from the submenu
  choices. Making a selection on the right side
  takes you to the iTunes store or a list of your
  synced media (**Figure 3.3**).

Figure 3.3
Accessing
the Movies
submenu.

PRESS SELECT/PLAY/PAUSE...   ...TO ACCESS A CATEGORY'S SELECTIONS.

- Press Menu when you want to go back to a previous menu screen, or to bring up the dual-pane menu.

- Press the Previous/Rewind and Next/Fast-forward buttons to move between menu panes, change songs, or skip within a movie.

tip   If you're a few steps within a section, such as Movies, pressing the Menu button brings you back to the previous screen. However, pressing and holding the Menu button for a few seconds will display the dual-pane menu from anywhere within the navigation.

When you see a greater-than symbol (>) to the right of a list item, another screen of options is available. If you don't see that, pressing Select/Play/Pause on the list item performs an action, such as playing back songs in Shuffle mode. Some list items display in gray, which means you'll have to activate a setting in order to access them (such as Parental Controls).

tip   Since Apple ships remotes with many of its products, keeping track of them can be difficult. My low-tech-but-effective solution is to wrap a colored rubber band around one (**Figure 3.4**). That also keeps the remote from skidding across the table.

Figure 3.4
My low-tech
remote-sorting
system.

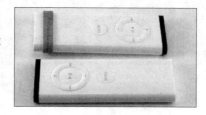

There's an initial bit of interface confusion for people who aren't accustomed to this iPod-style navigation. When you see a list item with a greater-than symbol (>), the logical choice would be to press the right-facing Next/Fast-forward button to get to the next screen, but that's not the case. It's a little nutty, and I see people make this "mistake" on the iPod all the time. But then again, Apple has sold 100 million iPods, so I think people get the hang of it pretty quickly.

tip **Because it uses infrared light, the Apple Remote needs a line of sight to the Apple TV to work. However, that doesn't always mean it has to be pointed directly at the Apple TV. Maybe I'm surrounded by a preponderance of shiny objects, but my remote seems to work no matter where I'm pointing it. Distance is also a factor: Make sure you're within 30 feet of the Apple TV.**

Pair the remote

If you own another Apple product that came with its own Apple remote, such as a recent Mac or an Apple Universal Dock (for use with an iPod and iPhone), and if that device is nearby, the Apple TV's remote might be activating it. My wife kept getting perplexed when her MacBook (on the other side of the room, even) would suddenly kick into Apple's Front Row software.

To remedy this infrared overlap, pair each remote to its respective device. On the Apple TV, do the following:

1. Press the Menu button to call up the floating main menu.

2. In the left pane, scroll down to Settings and press the Select/Play/Pause button. Then scroll to and select General to open the General Settings screen.

3. Scroll down to Pair Remote.

Figure 3.5
Remote paired.

4. Press Select/Play/Pause. After a second or two, an icon of the remote appears with a lock symbol above it (**Figure 3.5**). The Apple TV now responds only to that remote.

The remote will, however, still affect the other devices, so you should pair them, too.

1. Position the Apple Remote near the infrared receiver of the computer or iPod.

2. Press and hold the Menu and Next/Fast-forward buttons for six seconds. On the Mac, the remote icon appears in the center of the screen with a lock symbol above it to indicate pairing.

One easy way to tell if you're using the wrong Apple Remote is to look at the status light on the Apple TV. It flashes white when you use the paired remote, and amber when you use any other remote.

Unpair the remote

If you need to use a different remote, you can easily disassociate a paired remote. Go to the General Settings screen on the Apple TV and choose Unpair Remote. The icon returns with a broken chain symbol.

To unpair a remote from a Mac, go to System Preferences and open the Security preferences pane. Click the Unpair button at the bottom of the window. If you never intend to use a remote with your Mac, click the box labeled Disable remote control infrared receiver.

Lost the remote?

As you've seen, the Apple Remote is tiny—almost too tiny. I can imagine couches around the world subsisting on a steady diet of Apple Remotes. If yours gets lost somehow, or stops working altogether, you can buy a replacement from Apple for $19 or use one from another device. (Or, if you've been looking for a reason to buy a new Mac, think of it as buying a replacement remote that happens to come with a computer!) To make it work with your Apple TV that's been paired with another remote, press and hold the Menu and Previous/Rewind buttons for six seconds. The original pairing is discarded, and you can then pair the new remote.

tip **Third-party remote controls, such as Logitech's Harmony remotes (www.logitech.com), can also be programmed to work with the Apple TV.**

I'd like to go on about the rest of the interface's complexities, but there aren't any. We'll cover scrolling through lists and sections of the iTunes store in the upcoming chapters.

There are, however, a few more interface elements I want to look at here that affect your general usage of the Apple TV.

General Settings

These items don't fall into a neat category, and in fact, you may never need them. But, you never know. You can find these options by choosing Settings from the left side of the main menu, and then choosing General.

About

The About screen displays basic information about your Apple TV, broken out into general categories.

About the device

The first five items tell you the Apple TV's name (as defined when you set up syncing), hard drive capacity and available disk space, serial number, and version of the software that's running the show (**Figure 3.6**).

Figure 3.6
The About screen.

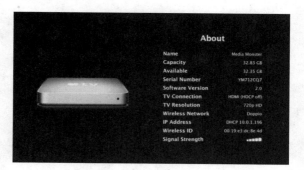

Network

The last items describe the state of the network. If you're connected to a wireless network, the name of the network is displayed, along with the assigned IP address. The Wireless ID code is how the Apple TV's hardware is identified on the network, while Signal Strength gives you an idea of whether it's running into interference. If an Ethernet cable is plugged in, you see only the IP address and the Ethernet ID code.

iTunes Store

Here you can change your location to another country's iTunes Store (if you have an account with a foreign iTunes store) as well as sign into or out of an iTunes account. See Chapter 4 for more on using the iTunes Store.

Update Software

Choose this option to manually check for available software updates over the Internet.

Language

Choose this option to change the language that's used by the interface. Practice your French skills!

Legal

Oh, you knew this would be here, and most people probably won't read it. But you'd be surprised at how entertaining the GNU license wording can be.

Reset Settings

To get back to the factory default settings, go to this screen, which offers three options.

- **CANCEL.** This is the "what am I doing here?" option that takes you back to the Settings screen.

- **RESET SETTINGS.** Choosing this option rolls your settings back to the factory defaults while keeping your connection, network, and sync settings.

- **FACTORY RESTORE.** This command wipes the Apple TV clean and takes you back to the state when you first unboxed the device. This is a good option for troubleshooting (see Chapter 10). If you bought a device with software version 1.0 or 1.1 and upgraded to 2.0, this option kicks the Apple TV back to the original version.

The Screen Saver

One downside to high-definition plasma televisions is that images can "burn in" if they remain static, leaving a ghostly impression. To prevent that, and to make the Apple TV more appealing to watch if it's playing music or otherwise not doing something visual, a screen saver begins after a few minutes.

Settings

To view the screen saver options, choose Settings from the left side of the main menu, and then choose Screen Saver on the right (**FIGURE 3.7**).

Figure 3.7
The screen
saver options.

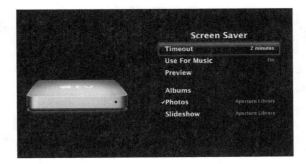

Timeout

Press the Select/Play/Pause button to choose a
period of inactive time after which the screen saver
starts: 2, 5, 10, 15, or 30 minutes, or Never to prevent it
from activating at all.

tip Disabling the screen saver by choosing Never as the
timeout doesn't mean your screen is at risk. The Apple
TV makes a point of moving objects around (such as
song information) to prevent burn-in.

Use for Music

Set this option to On to activate the screen saver
while music is playing. If it's set to Off, the Apple TV
displays only the song's album art and basic information (see Chapter 6).

Preview

Choose this item to see how the screen saver will
appear, without waiting for the timer to kick in.

The next three settings determine which screen saver to play; a check mark to the left indicates which one is active.

Albums

The Apple TV grabs the album art from your music collection and displays the images as if they were floating up to the sky. Every 30 seconds or so, the tableau spins on an axis to further ward off burn-in (**Figure 3.8**).

tip Even if you haven't synchronized music from your PC to the Apple TV, you can still choose Albums—the album art is culled wirelessly from iTunes on your computer. However, if that computer is put to sleep (or if it's a laptop that leaves the house), you'll end up with just a black screen.

Figure 3.8
Album artwork displayed as the screen saver.

Photos

The default screen saver, Photos, acts just like Albums but with photos. A selection of flower photographs is built into the Apple TV, but you can use your own synced photos. Or, you can choose to view photo albums stored online at either a .Mac Web Gallery or Flickr (**FIGURE 3.9**). (See Chapter 7 for more information on how to set up photo syncing, accessing online albums, and viewing slideshows.)

Figure 3.9
Choose the source for screen saver photos.

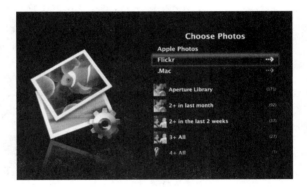

Slideshow

Where Photos and Albums float overlapping images of multiple sizes up from the bottom of your screen, Slideshow displays just a single photo at a time. You can modify the amount of time they appear on screen, as well as transitions and use of the Ken Burns Effect (which pans and zooms each photo across the screen) using the Settings found under the Photos section (see Chapter 7).

Video Settings

Before you sit down to watch a movie or TV episode, you can toggle a few options by selecting Video from the Settings submenu.

Closed Captioning

Press Select/Play/Pause to toggle between on and off. Even if you have Closed Captioning turned on, however, not all videos provided by studios to Apple include closed caption information.

TV Resolution

Selecting this item brings you to a screen with a list of available resolutions. When you first connect the Apple TV, it detects the resolutions your television is capable of displaying and chooses one automatically. If you're not happy with the appearance, or if the wrong one was chosen, pick another from this list.

HDMI Output

The HDMI Output setting affects how bright the interface appears—on some televisions, the text may seem blindingly white and object glows seem radioactive. The RGB High setting can also lend a bluish cast to the entire screen, washing out pure black areas. Press Select/Play/Pause on this setting to toggle between RGB High, RGB Low, and Auto.

 The main menu includes a few other settings, which I cover in their respective chapters: Downloads (Chapter 4), Audio (Chapter 6), and Computers (Chapter 8).

4

Buy and Rent Media

Before the Apple TV became public, people speculated on what an Apple-designed TV accessory would be like. Everyone assumed Apple would add the capabilities of a TiVo, letting you record broadcast television for playback later.

Realize, this doesn't happen with most companies. No one is idly speculating about how HP is going to improve kitchen appliances. But when Apple stepped out of the "computer" box by releasing the iPod (which wasn't the first digital music player by a long shot), people started asking, "What else can Apple do?" And the real unspoken question was, "What else can Apple do *better*?" So, an Apple television box would naturally control the content that's already coming into the television, right?

Well, people tend to forget that Apple is a profit-driven company, which, coincidentally, had already begun to sell movies and TV shows online through the iTunes Store. Why record something for free when you can buy it for less than the cost of a DVD? Maybe you prefer not to subscribe to cable or satellite TV service, or Netflix just takes too long. Whatever the reason, the iTunes Store is a direct line to your computer and, by extension, your Apple TV.

Buying or renting content from the iTunes Store isn't the exclusive way to get it onto your Apple TV; Chapter 9 covers the methods of ripping DVDs and converting your own edited movies to formats the Apple TV can read. But for some people, it's easier (and sometimes faster) to just purchase something from the iTunes Store.

In this chapter, I cover the two methods of buying media from Apple: on your computer using iTunes (for synchronizing to the Apple TV later), and buying and renting directly on the Apple TV itself.

Enter the iTunes Store

Figure 4.1
The iTunes
Store icon.

The iTunes Store exists on the Internet, but you can't get there using a Web browser. Instead, launch iTunes and look for the iTunes Store icon in the left column (**Figure 4.1**). When you click it, the store appears in place of your music library in the main area of the window (**Figure 4.2**).

Most of what you see are current promotions, new releases, and top-selling items in each category.

Figure 4.2
The iTunes Store.

 tip Double-click the iTunes Store icon to make the store appear in a separate window.

Browse for content

The store interface is ripe for browsing, so feel free to click away. If you want to be more directed, click a category in the iTunes Store box at the upper-left corner of the screen. That takes you to a similar screen containing just the type of content you clicked.

Figure 4.3
The directed Browse link.

QUICK LINKS

Browse
Power Search
Account
Buy iTunes Gifts

You can also browse the store in a less flashy, but more directed, interface. To locate an item, do the following:

1. In the Quick Links box at the upper-right, click the Browse link (**Figure 4.3**). This takes you to a category list of the store's offerings (**Figure 4.4**).

Figure 4.4
The iTunes Store
in Browse mode.

2. Choose a category from the iTunes Store column
(such as TV Shows).

3. In the next column, click a genre to narrow your
selection. If you're browsing podcasts, the column
lists podcast categories.

4. Depending on the media you choose, other
columns may appear, such as TV show titles,
subgenre, and artist. Click the items to narrow
the field until you see a list of media files in the
lower half of the screen.

Search for content

Figure 4.5
Search iTunes
Store field.

If you know what you're looking for, such as a movie's
name or the title (or partial title) of a song, type it
into the iTunes search field, which is labeled Search
iTunes Store when the store is active (**Figure 4.5**).
Press Enter to perform the search. A split screen
appears with the results categorized at the top and
listed at the bottom (**Figure 4.6**).

When you start typing in the search field, iTunes begins
to suggest relevant names and titles, and the list
narrows as you type more.

Figure 4.6
Search results
for the text
michael clayton.

Clicking items in the top portion takes you to more information. For example, clicking an album name displays the album with a full track list and notes, while clicking an artist name shows all albums by that artist.

As you peruse the store's wares, a set of buttons above the main screen indicate where you are (**Figure 4.7**). Clicking the Home button (with the house icon) takes you back to the main storefront. Clicking the category and genre buttons displays similar items. And the Back and Forward buttons step you through items you've already seen.

Figure 4.7
You won't get lost in the aisles with this handy navigation.

tip **Keep an eye out for free stuff. Yes, free! In addition to a Single of the Week, the store usually offers several other free songs and videos for you to try. Look for the Free on iTunes box on the main iTunes Store screen.**

Preview any store item by double-clicking it in the list at the bottom of the screen. Most previews are 30 seconds long; audiobooks are 90 seconds long; and movies play the film's theatrical trailer.

Power Search

For a more specific search, click the Power Search link in the Quick Links box. This option leads you to a form with multiple search fields (**FIGURE 4.8**), so you can locate all movies in the iTunes catalog directed by Spike Lee or starring Johnny Depp and produced by Jerry Bruckheimer.

Figure 4.8
Power Search.

Buy from iTunes

The iTunes Store offers two ways to purchase songs and videos: Buy them directly, or add them to a shopping cart to buy later. In either case, you need to have an account with Apple, which is used not only to charge your credit card but also to mark the media as belonging to you.

Set up an iTunes account

When you buy your first item, the store asks you to log in. However, it's just as easy to sign in beforehand and get everything set up. Here's how:

1. In the iTunes Store, click the Sign In button at the upper-right corner.

2. If you already have an Apple account (such as from the .Mac service) or AOL account, enter your Apple ID or AOL screen name and password in the fields provided and click the Sign In button (**Figure 4.9**).

Figure 4.9
Sign in to the iTunes Store.

If this is your first time here, click the Create New Account button. After accepting the terms and conditions, you'll be asked to provide a valid email address, a password, and credit card information.

Once you're signed in, the Sign In button in the store interface changes to display your Apple ID.

Buy now

Figure 4.10
Downloading
purchased item.

Apple apparently believes in instant gratification, because once you're signed in you can buy anything with the click of a button. In the list of items that appears when you're browsing or searching, click the Buy (Song, Movie, Episode, and so on) button. Your credit card is charged and the item is downloaded to your computer (**Figure 4.10**).

Shopping cart

If you'd prefer to load up before purchasing, you can choose to use a shopping cart. Choose Preferences from the iTunes menu (Mac) or the Edit menu (Windows), and click the Store tab. Then, click the Buy using a Shopping Cart radio button.

Figure 4.11
The Shopping
Cart.

A new Shopping Cart item appears in the Store section of the left-hand column in iTunes (**Figure 4.11**), and in the store itself, the Buy buttons become Add buttons. When you're ready to purchase, click Shopping Cart and then click the Buy Now button to start downloading the material.

Get a TV Show Season Pass

Earlier, I mentioned that you might not subscribe to cable or satellite TV service. Although for lots of people that idea sounds unthinkable, several of my friends prefer to get their television using the iTunes à la carte model.

But while you can buy episodes individually, it's easier and less expensive to purchase a show's Season Pass. For about $35 (depending on the show), you can download all episodes in a show's season—including ones that haven't yet aired. Each new episode appears on iTunes the day after it's broadcast.

tip **A Season Pass is also good for frequent travelers who want to keep current on their favorite shows.**

To purchase a season pass, navigate to the show you want and click the Buy/Add Season Pass button. When a new episode appears, Apple sends an email notifying you that it's available. Choose Check for Purchases from the Store menu, or sign in to your account and click the Manage Passes button, to download the latest.

tip **The Manage Passes screen is also where you can enable or disable email notification when new episodes appear.**

To bypass that step, go to the iTunes Preferences, click the Store tab, and enable "Automatically download prepurchased content." iTunes will regularly check to see if any new episodes are available for your shows and download them in the background.

Get a TV Show Multi-Pass

The Season Pass is good for shows with weekly episodes, but what if you want to catch every episode of a daily show, such as *The Colbert Report*? A Multi-Pass gives you the latest episode plus the next 15.

You also have the option to turn on auto-renewal, in which case your credit card will be charged for the next 16 episodes once you've reached the end of your previous Multi-Pass collection.

 After you purchase a Season Pass or Multi-Pass, you can't cancel it. Choose wisely, grasshopper.

iTunes Authorizations

Apple's scheme for thwarting piracy is to protect nearly every song and video in the iTunes Store using a system called FairPlay. Each file is encoded with your account email and requires that the computer you're attempting to play it on is authorized by you. You can authorize a total of five computers at any time. When you attempt to play a song or video on an unauthorized machine, iTunes asks for the Apple ID and password corresponding to your account, and then checks its database at Apple HQ to make sure you haven't hit your quota.

You can deauthorize a computer at any time—in fact, if you ever retire or sell a computer, make sure you deauthorize iTunes first so it won't count against your authorizations. If you run into a situation where you need to deauthorize a machine but can't (if its hard drive went out in a puff of smoke, for example), and you've reached the maximum number of authorizations, you'll find a Deauthorize All button in your iTunes account information. You can use that option only once per year, however.

The Apple TV, fortunately, does not count as one of your five authorized computers.

Rent Movies Using iTunes

Instead of spending $10 or more to own a movie that you'll likely watch once and occupies more than a gigabyte of space on your hard disk, you can rent it. No waiting for Netflix envelopes to arrive or fighting traffic on a Friday night to discover the movie you want has already been taken at your local retail rental behemoth. While some movies are still purchase-only, you'll see more and more with an additional Rent Movie button placed above the Buy/Add Movie button (**Figure 4.12**).

Figure 4.12
Renting a movie from the iTunes Store.

Figure 4.13
Rented Movies category.

Renting a movie is just as easy as buying one, but with a slight wrinkle. Clicking the Rent Movie button engages the transaction, even if you've selected the shopping cart method for purchasing. You'll also find that a new Rented Movies item appears in the Store section of iTunes (**Figure 4.13**).

The minimal ground rules for rentals are:

- You have 30 days to begin watching a rented movie from when you first download it.

- Once you begin watching the movie, the clock starts ticking faster—you have 24 hours to finish watching it before the movie file is deleted.

 tip **If you're in the middle of watching a movie at the end of its 24-hour window, you can finish watching it as long as it's still active. Additionally, if you pause a movie before it's expiry point, you can start it back up after the 24-hour window has closed. But there's a catch: You have to keep the movie window open. If you close it, then you'll have to re-rent it to find out who wins the big game (here's a hint—it's usually the good guys).**

 note **If you're using Time Machine to back up your Mac, the file is also automatically deleted from your archives.**

Transfer Rented Movies to the Apple TV

To watch the rental on your TV, you must first manually move it there over your network.

1. Open iTunes on your computer and select your Apple TV from the Devices list in the left column.

2. Click the Movies tab; a Rented Movies section has been placed above the Sync section (**Figure 4.14**).

3. Click the Move button. iTunes contacts the iTunes Store and sets the Apple TV as the new location.

4. Click the Apply button to perform a sync and transfer the movie file to the Apple TV.

Figure 4.14
Move the rental
from iTunes to
your Apple TV.

 To maximize your entertainment mobility, you can transfer the rental from iTunes to an iPhone or an iPod that's compatible with Apple's movie rentals (the iPod classic, iPod touch, and the wide-bodied, third-generation iPod nano). You'll have to perform the same Move procedure after selecting the iPod/iPhone in the Devices list. And to get it back to the Apple TV, you'll have to move it back to your iTunes library (where the file will be found in the Rented Movies item in the left-hand column) and then do another move to the Apple TV.

Buy and Rent Media Using the Apple TV

Hey, wait a second, the Apple TV is connected to the Interent—you don't need no stinkin' iTunes! With version 2.0 of the Apple TV software, you can purchase media and rent movies, directly from the Apple TV.

 Check out Apple TV Junkie (www.appletvjunkie.com), a Web site that's tracking all the new movies and TV shows that are available on the Apple TV.

tip If you were paying careful attention to Figure 4.12 earlier, you saw that HD movie rentals are an option—but solely to owners of Apple TV. HD titles cost an extra $1.

Browse for Content

The Apple TV provides complete access to the three main sections of the iTunes Store—Movies, TV Shows, and Music—as well as Music Videos found within Music. (Podcasts are also available, but I cover them in Chapter 6.)

Here's how to get started:

1. Press the Menu button on the Apple Remote.

2. On the left side of the menu, select one of the media types by pressing Select/Play/Pause.

3. Scroll to one of the submenu choices (such as All HD under Movies or Top TV Shows), and press Select/Play/Pause.

4. Scroll through the list that appears on the next screen, then press Select/Play/Pause to view a title.

Search for Content

The top-level sections of the iTunes Store are great for browsing new releases and popular titles, but if you know what you're looking for, you can search for it directly.

1. Press the Menu button to call up the main menu, choose the media type you want to search, then select Search from the right pane of the menu.

note   Unlike the iTunes Store on your PC, where you'll see search results from all available media, the Apple TV does not perform cross-media searches.

2. Use the remote to scroll through the alpha-numeric palette and press Select/Play/Pause to make a selection. (Choose the **#+=** button at the bottom to switch to a palette of special characters.) A list of artists and titles appears on the right side of the screen (**FIGURE 4.15**).

Figure 4.15
Searching for movies also locates actors and directors.

3. Continue making selections to narrow your choice, then press the Next/Fast-forward button to jump to the list of search results.

4. Press Select/Play/Pause to view media available for purchase or rent, then Select/Play/Pause again to view a title.

Buy or Rent

Now that you've found what you want, here's how to get the media onto your Apple TV.

Movies

Figure 4.16
Rental buttons.

After selecting your title, you'll find an overview page with a short synopsis, movie rating, and details such as actors, directors and movie length. You then have two or three options: the ubiquitous Preview button plays the film's theatrical trailer, and one or two Rent buttons correspond to SD (standard-definition) and HD versions (**Figure 4.16**).

 Press the Menu up/scroll (+) button to view the full-synopsis; press it again to see the details; and press it a third time to return to the combined details.

To rent a movie, do the following:

1. Select one of the two rental options and press Select/Play/Pause.

2. On the confirmation screen, select OK to move on.

3. The Apple TV contacts the iTunes Store and a Rented Movies screen appears, collecting all of the movies you've rented with the download progress appearing below the film's poster.

 Downloading video is bandwidth intensive. If the Apple TV is swamping your Internet connection, you can pause the download: At the main menu, choose Settings > Downloads; highlight the download in progress and press Select/Play/Pause to pause the transfer.

After the movie has downloaded a bit, a message appears telling you the movie is ready to watch. You don't have to wait for the entire movie file to download before you begin watching (depending on the speed of your Internet connection, of course).

Press Select/Play/Pause to begin watching immediately (remembering you have just 24 hours to
complete the viewing), or press the Menu button to
watch later (**FIGURE 4.17**). If you do begin to watch
your film, you'll see how much the movie has downloaded on the progress bar at the bottom of the
screen (press Select/Play/Pause to call it up; it will
disappear again after two seconds). For more about
watching movies, see Chapter 5.

Figure 4.17
Once you start
watching, you
have 24 hours to
finish viewing
the movie.

| tip | After you've rented a movie, you can go about your business browsing through the Apple TV. A new submenu option under Movies appears in the main menu (called Rented Movies), enabling you to easily return to your rental. |

TV Shows

When you select a TV Show, you're presented with a
list of available single episodes to buy (no renting)
as well as an option to buy all the episodes you see
in one fell swoop (**FIGURE 4.18**). If more than one

season is available, you'll see an option for that with a greater-than symbol (>). Scroll through the list and view the details for each episode (including original air date and length).

Figure 4.18
Choose individual episodes, or buy all at once.

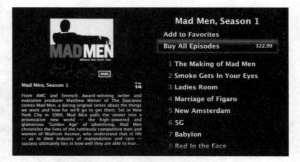

To make a purchase, press Select/Play/Pause to get to the overview screen, then navigate to the Buy button and press Select/Play/Pause. At the confirmation screen, just select OK and begin downloading.

You'll need to purchase Season Passes and Multi-Passes using iTunes on your PC, as the Apple TV only offers the capability to buy just currently available episodes, not yet-to-be-released episodes.

If you're not ready to commit to buying all episodes from a season, choose Add to Favorites at the top of the episode list. This sends an icon for the show to the Favorites collection (found under TV Shows in the main menu), enabling you to quickly scan recently added episodes.

As with Movies, you can begin watching a TV show shortly after it begins downloading, or return to it later by selecting My TV Shows from the main menu. For more on watching TV Shows, see Chapter 5.

Music

The purchasing process for Music is similar to TV Shows. Whether a full album or just an E.P., most titles come with several songs, so you get the option to buy the entire album at the top of the list. Otherwise, you can select an individual song, choose the Buy button on the overview page, and go through the confirmation screen to buy the song.

Unlike Movies and TV Shows, the Apple TV won't inform you that your new music is ready for listening. You'll need to find your new purchases by visiting My Music on the main menu (under Music in the left pane). And when you next sync to your PC, you'll find a new Purchased item (with the name of your Apple TV) in the Store section of the left-hand column in iTunes (**Figure 4.19**).

Figure 4.19
Purchases made on the Apple TV get synced to iTunes.

tip

While there isn't a Recently Added playlist waiting for you on the Apple TV, it already exists in iTunes as a Smart Playlist: Sync it to the Apple TV to get to your new tunes easily (see Chapter 8).

5

Watch Movies, TV Shows, and YouTube

Okay, the Apple TV is hooked up, networked, synchronized with a computer, and ready to deliver entertainment you've purchased from the iTunes Store (either from your PC or the Apple TV itself) or provided yourself (see Chapter 9).

And, as we learned in Chapter 1, it's connected to a *widescreen TV*. More than likely, your TV is of generous size—maybe it's not a 102-inch monstrosity featured at events such as the yearly Consumer Electronics Show, but larger than the no-name TV/VCR combo that came home from college with you.

What to do? Let's fill that screen with some video!

Screen a Movie

Pop the popcorn, fluff up the couch pillows, dim the lights, and settle in.

Watch movie trailers

Call me traditional, but I like the experience of seeing movie trailers before a feature film, just like in a theater. In this case, however, I don't have to sit through annoying commercials, and I get to choose which trailers to watch. The Apple TV connects to the Internet and can download trailers for movies that are currently screening in or coming soon to theaters. Do the following:

1. From the Apple TV's main menu, choose Movies on the left and then Trailers on the right.

2. You can choose between two sets of trailers (**Figure 5.1**). Select from the list of standard definition titles that appears, or choose the HD Trailers option at the top and select from that list.

Figure 5.1 Highlighting a title gives you more information about the film.

tip If you keep a title highlighted for a couple of seconds (depending on the speed of your Internet connection), the large poster image on the left gets replaced by a smaller one as well as a short (usually truncated) synopsis and movie details.

note Remember, you can also watch trailers for movies featured in the iTunes Store by selecting the Preview button on the movie's overview page. And, if the trailer is compelling, immediate gratification is yours.

Figure 5.2
Progress bar.

3. Press Select/Play/Pause to start downloading the trailer. A progress bar appears at the bottom of the screen (**FIGURE 5.2**). The spinning cursor indicates that video is downloading, while the solid blue line tells you how much of the video has transferred. The black triangle is the playhead, which indicates where you are within the video.

After enough video has buffered (and again, that will depend on your Internet connection), the trailer starts playing (**FIGURE 5.3**). When it finishes, you're taken back to the list of trailers.

Figure 5.3
The trailer plays after enough video is downloaded.

tip

Even if you have a widescreen television, the video may appear letterboxed, showing black bars above and below the movie image. While most widescreen TVs have an aspect ratio of 1.78:1 (more commonly referred to as 16:9), film is generally projected in a shorter 1.85:1 aspect ratio that emphasizes width (and allows cinematographers to really capture scenic vistas). Do not attempt to adjust the picture; we control the horizontal and the vertical.

Choose a movie

Okay, enough with the movies you can't yet watch in their entirety—what about the ones on the Apple TV's hard drive? With version 2.0 of the Apple TV's software, purchased and rented movies are found in two different locations. For movies you've purchased from the iTunes Store on your PC or have created yourself (either via iMovie or encoded from one of your DVDs), follow these steps.

Choose a purchased movie

1. Press the Menu button to access the Apple TV's main menu.

2. Choose Movies and then select My Movies in the right pane.

3. Scroll down the list to select the movie you want to watch. As with trailers, information about it appears to the left, including the movie's duration (**FIGURE 5.4**). Movies that didn't come from the iTunes Store display the first frame of video as the preview image.

Figure 5.4
Browsing
My Movies.

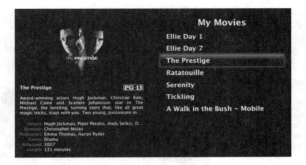

4. Press Select/Play/Pause to start the movie.

As with browsing in the iTunes Store, press the Menu up/scroll (+) button to view all of the truncated details.

A movie file doesn't need to be on your Apple TV's hard drive in order for you to watch it—it can be streamed over your network from iTunes on your PC. But if you aren't seeing the movie you're looking for, check that the Apple TV and your computer are both connected to the network and that iTunes is running. Also check the sync settings in iTunes to make sure your movie isn't being excluded from the sync process if you want to watch a file without accessing your PC. You can find more about synchronizing and streaming in Chapter 8, but for now I'm assuming the movies you want have been synced from your computer or downloaded directly.

Choose a rented movie

1. Press the Menu button to access the Apple TV's main menu.

2. Choose Movies and then select Rented Movies in the right pane.

3. On the Rented Movies screen, highlight the icon of the rental you want to watch (**Figure 5.5**).

Figure 5.5
The Rented Movies repository.

Figure 5.6
Press to play.

4. On the next screen, where the Play button is highlighted, press Select/Play/Pause to start the movie (**Figure 5.6**).

You'll need to make sure the Apple TV is connected to the Internet, as it needs to authorize that the movie is good to go. Once it makes a successful handshake with the iTunes Store, the movie will start to play.

If you pause the rental and go back to its overview screen, you'll find a Delete button has been added, allowing you to manually trash it. But don't worry about that—the file automagically disappears from the Apple TV's hard drive, freeing up precious space for more movies.

Watch a movie

Now, while I enjoy going out to see a movie—and there's nothing like seeing a film with a crowd of other moviegoers—screening a movie at home does have its advantages. I can pause in the middle to get something from the refrigerator, watch a particularly good scene again, or skip past boring sections.

Pause and resume

To halt playback, press the Select/Play/Pause button. Press the button again to start playing again.

If you pause a movie and then move on to other areas of the Apple TV, when you return to the movie later you'll be given the option of resuming play from that same spot or starting over from the beginning (FIGURE 5.7).

Figure 5.7
Continuing playback. I love the blurred frame that highlights the text.

If you start watching a rented film and then move it to another compatible device (such as an iPhone), the movie restarts from the beginning rather than the paused location. Hopefully this is just a bug.

Jump back or jump ahead

Movies from the iTunes Store include chapter markers,
just as you'd find on a DVD, that let you skip ahead
to specific scenes. To jump to the next chapter, press
the Next/Fast-forward button once. To jump back
one chapter, press the Previous/Rewind button once.
When you do, the chapter name appears above the
progress bar at the bottom of the screen (**Figure 5.8**).

Figure 5.8
Moving
between
chapter
markers.

If the movie does not include chapter markers, such
as a video you've created or ripped from a DVD,
pressing the Next/Fast-forward and Previous/Rewind
buttons jumps ahead or back incrementally. The
length of the jump depends on the duration of the
movie; a two-hour feature, for example, jumps about
seven minutes per button press.

Skip in 10-second increments

For more precise searching, you can rewind or
forward the video in 10-second blocks. Here's how:

1. Press the Select/Play/Pause button to pause the
   movie.

2. Press the Next/Fast-forward button to skip ahead 10 seconds, or press the Previous/Rewind button to skip back 10 seconds.

Fast-forward or rewind

Instead of jumping around, you may want to quickly scan the video at three different speeds.

1. Press and hold the Previous/Rewind or Next/Fast-forward button to speed up playback.

Figure 5.9
Fast-forwarding speed indicator.

The triangular play icon at the far left of the progress bar changes into a set of three triangles that indicate the speed (**Figure 5.9**). The longer you hold down the button, the faster playback will be; three white triangles is the fastest speed.

2. Press the Select/Play/Pause button again to resume normal playback.

tip You can also change the reviewing speed without keeping the button held down. Press Previous/Rewind or Next/Fast-forward and hold it long enough to start the accelerated playback. Then, let go of the button—the quick-scan continues. Press the button once to switch to the next-fastest speed. For example, if you're fast-forwarding at the first fast speed (one triangle), pressing the Next/Fast-forward button once speeds up to the next speed (two triangles). You can also go back one speed by pressing the Previous/Rewind button. Lastly, pressing the Next/Fast-forward button at the fastest speed (three triangles) kicks it back down to the first fast speed (one triangle).

Slow motion

In *Pirates of the Caribbean: The Curse of the Black Pearl*, is that a crew member in a cowboy hat standing on the deck of the pirate ship? (Yep.) It's easy to catch gaffes like that by slowing the playback:

1. Press the Select/Play/Pause button to pause the movie.

2. Press and hold the Previous/Rewind or Next/ Fast-forward button to play back in slow motion. As with speeding up the video, holding down the button (or pressing it again once playback resumes) changes the speed of the slow-motion playback.

3. Press the Select/Play/Pause button again to return to normal speed.

When you engage sped-up or slow-motion playback, the audio is muted.

Did you know you can get free HD video from Apple? An increasing number of video podcasts are offered in HD formats. In iTunes, click the Podcasts item in the sidebar and then click the Podcast Directory button.

Watch a TV Show

You won't be surprised to learn that watching a TV show is just like watching a movie. The same controls work for playing, pausing, and reviewing video. What's different is how the Apple TV organizes the shows and their episodes.

tip

Because there are no chapter markers in a TV Show video, pressing the Next/Fast-forward or Previous/Rewind button only jumps incrementally.

From the Apple TV's main menu, select My TV Shows and press Select/Play/Pause. Here you'll see a list of all the television show titles you've purchased (**Figure 5.10**).

Figure 5.10
The My TV Shows screen, with Show view active.

The list can be sorted two different ways: by Show and by Date.

Show view

The Show view is the default and is helpful when you subscribe to several shows because it groups episodes together by series.

1. If the Show view is not already active, press the Next/Fast-forward button. It doesn't matter which item is selected in the list.

   In this view, each show is given its own line with a greater-than symbol (>) indicating when more than one episode is available. When a show contains unwatched episodes, a blue sphere appears next to the show title.

2. Press Select/Play/Pause to choose a show.

3. On the next screen, choose an episode name to watch it (**Figure 5.11**).

Figure 5.11
The episodes available for a particular show.

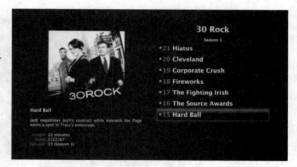

If you've finished watching an episode you purchased directly on the Apple TV, and you haven't synced yet with iTunes, select it in the list for a few seconds. You'll see a small trash can icon appears at the right, enabling you to delete the file manually before it gets transferred over to your PC on your next sync—handy if you have limited hard drive space on your PC.

Date view

In the Date view, each episode appears in the list, sorted by the date it was purchased.

1. Press the Previous/Rewind button to switch to the Date view.

Newest episodes show up at the top of the list, but there's a catch: Only the show name appears in the list. You need to highlight an episode and look at its information (in the lower left corner of the screen) to learn the episode name, number, and the date it first aired (**Figure 5.12**).

Figure 5.12
TV Shows
sorted by date.

2. Press Select/Play/Pause to start playing an episode.

The Date view sorts only by the date that episodes were purchased, which runs into sorting problems. If you're following along with a Season Pass or Multi-Pass, this isn't a big deal because the latest episode appears chronologically based on its original air date. But for shows that have already aired, there's no secondary sorting on either episode number or original air date. That leads to a list of Star Trek episodes, for example, that appear based on when they were added to iTunes—and since iTunes doesn't necessarily download them in order, you end up with a jumble. Sorting by Show instead gives you a season in reverse episode order (newest first), avoiding confusion.

tip When you begin to play an episode, the Apple TV considers it "watched" and removes the blue sphere icon, even if you didn't watch the whole thing. However, in terms of syncing, it's not completely "watched": with the sync option in iTunes set to sync only unwatched episodes, the partially-viewed one is still included (see Chapter 8). The blue icon indicates the item is *completely* unwatched; if you watch only part of the episode, the icon goes away because you've watched part of it. However, the episode remains on the list as unwatched because you've not watched it through to the end.

Closed Captioning

Some movies offered by iTunes include closed-captioning information, which displays dialog as subtitles for the benefit of people who are hard of hearing (or for when you're watching a movie where the accents are especially difficult to parse). To enable the Closed Captioning feature, do the following:

1. From the main menu, choose Settings in the left column and Video in the right column.

2. Select the Closed Captioning option and press Select/Play/Pause to toggle between Off and On.

 note Not all movies include this information, so even if Closed Captioning is enabled you won't see text subtitles if the data isn't there in the first place.

Watch YouTube Videos

One thing missing from the Apple TV is commercials. Happily (yes, bear with me), you can graze through a virtually unlimited supply of uploaded commercials, music videos, and scenes from movies and TV shows, as well as a wide assortment of user-generated content—from police chases to babies crawling—courtesy of YouTube.

Log In to Your Account

While you can view videos without having signed up as a YouTube user, you'll be able to access more YouTube features by choosing to Log In from the main menu. (If you don't have an account already set up, you'll have to do this from the YouTube Web site.)

1. Select YouTube in the left pane of the main menu, then Log In from the right, and press Select/Play/Pause.

2. Navigate the onscreen keyboard to enter your User Name and then your Password, selecting Done at the bottom of the screen each time.

3. On the next screen, you'll see Favorites and Subscriptions (other YouTube users you've chosen to follow). If videos are saved in either of those sections, you'll see a greater-than symbol (>). You can also choose to log out.

   To return to this screen later, choose My Account (which replaces Log In) at the main menu.

Oddly, while YouTube on the Apple TV provides access to your Favorites and Subscriptions in the My Account submenu, there's no option that collects the videos you've uploaded to your YouTube account (also referred to as your Channel). However, you can search for your account name or very specific tag (which you can enter into the video's details on the YouTube Web site). You won't have to enter this term every time you want to see your videos. Instead, choose the Recent Searches option on the Search screen and select the search you want to display.

Find and Play YouTube Videos

You can browse YouTube on the Apple TV much like you would on your computer. The submenu categories in the right pane of the main menu include Featured, Most Viewed, Most Recent, and Top Rated.

 The Most Viewed and Top Rated sections also allow you to choose from Today, This Week, and All Time. Press the Next/Fast-forward and Previous/Rewind buttons to move between time periods.

To view a YouTube video, do the following.

1. Select the category you want to browse (such as Favorites from your account screen or Top Rated from the main menu), and press Select/Play/Pause.

2. Use the Menu up/scroll (+) and Menu down/scroll (–) buttons to navigate the list. The details for each video appear on the left side of the screen (**Figure 5.13**).

3. Press Select/Play/Pause to start playing the video.

Figure 5.13
Browsing for
YouTube videos.

> **tip** The playback controls for YouTube videos are the same for watching TV Shows.

4. When the video ends, choose to Play Again (or Resume if you ended the video early by pressing the Menu button). Choose the Show More option to see more videos posted by that user, or browse through a list of related videos (**Figure 5.14**).

Figure 5.14
More YouTube
options.

5. If you're signed into your account, you can take advantage of Options by pressing Select/Play/Pause: Choose Rate this Video to add a 1- to 5-star rating on the next screen; save the video to your Favorites collection (or Remove it); or flag the video as having inappropriate content.

6. Press Menu to return to the previous screen, and press Menu again to return to the YouTube section you were browsing.

History

To easily return to a video, open the Apple TV's main menu and select History from the YouTube submenu. You'll find a list of the videos you've viewed on the Apple TV (even if you started downloading the video). If you choose a video to watch from your History, it gets placed at the top of the list.

Search

If you know what you're looking for, choose Search from the YouTube submenu on the Apple TV's main menu.

1. "Type" on the alpha-numeric keyboard using the Apple Remote. The selections change as you enter characters, narrowing your choices.

2. When you've found the right video(s), press the Next/Fast-forward button to jump to the list of search results (**Figure 5.15**). (Press Previous/Rewind to return to the keyboard.)

Figure 5.15
Performing a
YouTube search.

3. Navigate the list—details for each video appear
on the left, replacing the search keyboard.

4. Press Select/Play/Pause to play the selection.

5. At the end of the video (or if you pressed Menu to
stop viewing), choose Return to Search and then
press Select/Play/Pause (or just press Menu) to
return to the search list and keyboard.

Parental Controls

The Apple TV is a great portal to video and photos on
the Internet, but you may not want it to be a wide
open door to everything available online. Using the
Parental Controls features, you can control which
types of content are downloaded, choose minimum
allowed ratings for movies and television shows, and
make sure Junior doesn't rack up huge charges by
renting every HD movie available.

To enable Parental Controls, do the following:

1. From the main menu, select Settings in the left pane, then General on the right.

2. Navigate to Parental Controls and press Select/Play/Pause.

3. Select Turn on Parental Controls and press Select/Play/Pause. (You can navigate to the other grayed-out list items, but they won't become active until Parental Controls are turned on.)

4. On the next screen, create a passcode using the Menu up/scroll and Menu down/scroll buttons to select digits from each of the four numeric fields. Navigate between the digits by pressing the Next/Fast-forward and Previous/Rewind buttons on the remote.

5. When finished, choose Done and press Select/Play/Pause.

6. Wait, you're not finished—you get to reenter the same digits to confirm the passcode. If it doesn't match the first entry, you'll have to start over.

Make sure the passcode is something the parents of the house will easily remember, or write it down and hide it somewhere. If you forget the passcode, you'll have to restore the Apple TV to its factory settings.

Back in the Parental Controls screen, all the control options are now available to you (**Figure 5.16**)—as is an option for changing the passcode should your munchkins sleuth out your current code.

Figure 5.16
Parental
Controls.

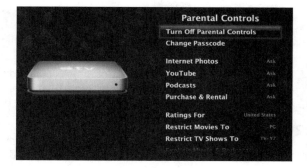

Permissions

With the first three options in the list—Internet Photos, YouTube, and Podcast—press the Select/Play/Pause button to toggle between the following three options:

- **ASK.** This is the default behavior for Parental Controls, and it requires the passcode to be entered in order to access one of these areas. For example, if you chose Most Viewed under YouTube from the main menu, the Enter Passcode screen would first appear.

- **SHOW.** Selecting this option provides unrestricted access to an area.

- **HIDE.** With this option, the menu item is removed from the main menu so that no one can access it.

The Purchase & Rental option lets you choose to **ASK** for the passcode after the confirmation screen for all purchases or rentals, or **ALLOW** purchases without passcode authorization.

Ratings

Choose limits on video and audio based on content ratings.

- **RATINGS FOR.** Choosing a country displays the ratings used in that market; toggle the options by pressing the Select/Play/Pause button. For this example, I'll stick to the United States.

- **RESTRICT MOVIES TO.** You have the standard MPAA ratings options of G, PG, PG-13, and R. If you choose G (safe for general audiences), any movie with a rating restriction above that would require a passcode entry. You can also select No to skip enforcing this control.

 I'm guessing Apple must deliberately not offer movies rated NC-17 through iTunes, since that rating is not available.

- **RESTRICT TV SHOWS TO.** Here you can choose from the spectrum of television content ratings, starting at TV-Y (suitable for all ages) and moving upward through TV-Y7, TV-G, TV-PG, and TV-14. Again, selecting one of these options requires the passcode to view a show with a higher rating. If you choose No, shows with a TV-MA rating can be viewed without restriction.

- **EXPLICIT MUSIC & PODCASTS.** With this option, you get two choices: Ask or Allow. By choosing Ask, any music (even if it's streamed from your PC) will bring up the passcode screen if a song or album has been labeled as Explicit.

6

Play Music, Podcasts, and Audiobooks

Music and television have always been separate experiences for me, mostly because my college bookshelf stereo system sounded much better than the so-so speakers in my old TV. But now, the speakers are pretty good in many widescreen televisions and I've set my audio/visual system so that the movies' sound comes through a home theater speaker system.

Given its easy-to-use visual interface, why *not* turn the Apple TV into the living room jukebox? It can play all your music and audiobooks and stay current on your favorite podcasts.

Play Music

From the Apple TV's main menu, choose Music in the left pane, choose My Music in the right, and then press Select/Play/Pause to switch to the My Music screen (**Figure 6.1**). You'll see a random selection of floating/rotating album covers on the left to enter-tain you. (Okay, so I'm easily entertained.)

Figure 6.1
The My Music
screen.

Choose a song

The list on the right side of the screen represents different methods of listing the contents of your iTunes music library.

Shuffle Songs

Before the MP3 age, the way to listen to a random selection of music involved either creating your own mix tape (which wasn't necessarily random) or buying a multidisc CD player that could load a disc, play a song at random, unload the disc, load another disc, play a song at random, and so forth.

From the My Music screen, scroll down to Shuffle Songs and press the Select/Play/Pause button. The Apple TV picks a song at random from your entire library and plays it.

 The Shuffle Songs feature ignores audiobooks and music videos.

Music Videos

Playing a music video is just like playing a movie or TV show, which I covered in Chapter 5. As with TV shows, the greater-than symbol (>) at the end of the line indicates a screen with more options, in this case a list of artists with music videos. Pressing Select on an artist's name takes you to a list of videos, and pressing Select on a video title plays it.

 Even though there's an All option at the top of the Music Videos screen, it only shows all the video titles collected together. But even from the All screen, you can only watch one music video at a time. The Apple TV won't start the next video when the last has ended—even if you've set up a music video playlist in iTunes. So much for having your own video jukebox playing in the background.

Playlists

When you choose Playlists from the Music menu, you can select one of the iTunes playlists from your computer. See "Set up playlists," later in this chapter, for more information.

Artists

Choose an artist's name to view a list of albums by that performer, which in turn leads to songs on the album. Press Select/Play/Pause to play the song you want to hear.

Albums

If you know the name of the album you want to listen to, choose Albums from the Music screen and scroll to the title. Choosing the album brings up a screen containing the album's songs; press Select on the first song to start playing the album.

 The lists correctly sort names by ignoring "The" and "A" in front of the title. So *The Crane Wife*, by The Decemberists, appears with the "C" albums, not the "T"s (and The Decemberists show up in the "D"s).

 When you get to an album's screen, you also have the option to shuffle the songs just from that album (as long as more than one song is available).

Songs

Every once in a while, I get a snippet of a song in my head that won't leave unless I hear the real thing. Go to the Songs screen to locate the song's title, and then press Select to start playing it (and hopefully banish it from the soundtrack loop in my brain).

 Whereas the iPod's interface places album and song titles that start with a number (such as "1234" by Feist) at the end of a list, the Apple TV places them up top.

Genres

Although people debate about assigning genres to music—is it wrong to categorize music according to some marketing label? And can an album be both "alternative" and "pop" or "rock" at the same time?—I find the classification most helpful when applied broadly. Selecting the Classical or Soundtrack genres, for example, significantly narrows my choices so I can find what I'm looking for faster.

Composers

Speaking of classical music, the Composers category is especially helpful when you know you want to listen to something by Bach, because most recordings assign the conductor or symphony's name to the Artist category. Choosing Composers leads to a list of composers, which in turn takes you to the albums and songs by that composer.

Audiobooks

Choose Audiobooks to bring up a list of authors of audiobooks, which leads to the book titles.

Scrolling

One challenge with any interface is how to easily navigate among hundreds or thousands of items.

As you'd guess, press the Menu-up/scroll (+) and Menu-down/scroll (–) buttons to scroll the lists. When you press and hold one of the buttons, the items scroll by faster until the words become a blur.

Thanks to persistence of vision, your eyes should still see which letter you're at in the alphabet (I find it helps to focus just on the first letter). Release the button when you get close to the item you want, which slows the scroll, and then press the buttons to fine-tune your selection.

The biggest annoyance when fast scrolling is that the selection box overshoots; for example, you could be looking for The Shins but end up at U2. To counteract the acceleration, when you release the held-down button, press the opposite scroll button once. The list will pop closer to your intended target.

This is one area where I'd like to see some of the recent iPod enhancements applied. The latest iPod interface displays a large letter to indicate where you are in the alphabet. Similarly, it would be helpful if the Apple TV had the capability to enter letters as a search term.

Play a song

As a song is playing, the Apple TV displays the album artwork, the song title in white, and the artist and album name below that in gray (**Figure 6.2**). A progress bar indicates how much time has elapsed and how much time remains. If you're playing in shuffle mode, you'll also see a crossed-arrow icon indicating the playback is random.

Figure 6.2
Stop, listen,
what's that
sound? A song
is playing.

Also noted is the song position: When playing in shuffle, song, or playlist modes, a number such as "6 of 1,232" tells you that the piece is listed as number 6 out of 1,232 total songs in your library; admittedly, that's not very helpful. However, when you're playing an album, the number can give you an idea of whether you're at the beginning or end of the album (such as "7 of 10").

note As noted in Chapter 3, pressing the Menu button takes you back one level in the menu hierarchy. When you press Menu during playback (let's say you want to find a different album), the song continues to play. However, music stops if you switch to one of the other areas (such as My TV Shows or even Settings).

While a song is playing, you can do the following:

- **PLAY/PAUSE.** Press the Select/Play/Pause button to pause and resume playback.

- **SCAN.** Press and hold the Previous/Rewind button to scan backward at high speed, or press and hold the Next/Fast-forward button to zip ahead. Unlike movie playback, there's only one speed for scanning through songs. However, song snippets play to help you get your bearings.

- **SKIP.** To skip to the previous or next song, press the Previous/Rewind or Next/Fast-forward button once.

tip Contravening common sense, the Menu-up and Menu-down buttons do not affect playback volume. I understand why—the TV or stereo is usually the device that dictates volume—but you'd think Apple would let you make an adjustment from the Apple Remote. Alas, no.

tip So, what are those buttons good for during playback? Press either one while the screen saver is running to bring up the Now Playing screen without taking action. Otherwise, pressing the Previous or Next button skips a song and the Select/Play/Pause button pauses or resumes the song while allowing the screen saver to continue running—a great trick for parties.

Now Playing

When a song is playing, a new item appears on the Music screen. Now Playing is a shortcut to view the current song and bypass the need to navigate through the artist/album hierarchy.

tip You can also get back to the current song by doing nothing. After a few seconds of inactivity, the Apple TV returns to the Now Playing screen.

Audio settings

The Apple TV includes two settings that affect all music playback. From the Apple TV's main menu, choose Settings in the left pane and then choose Audio in the right.

Repeat Music

Press the Select/Play/Pause button on this item to toggle its setting between Off and On. When enabled, an album or playlist will start over from the beginning after the last song is played. This feature doesn't affect single songs, however.

tip

Well, *by default* you can't loop a single song. To work around that limitation, go into iTunes and create a new playlist containing just that song (see "Set Up iTunes Playlists" on the next page). Then, instead of locating the song using the Song menu on the Apple TV, you can play just that playlist from the Playlists menu and listen to your favorite song over and over.

Sound Check

Due to the way music is mastered, some songs end up sounding softer or louder than others when you rip their CDs into iTunes. Sound Check attempts to even out the volume level so that you don't need to turn up the volume for a soft song and then get your ears blown out later by a loud song. Press Select/Play/Pause to toggle this feature between Off and On.

tip Although Sound Check seems like a great feature, I admit I don't use it. Perhaps my library has too much of a broad volume range, but I find that Sound Check makes everything in general too soft.

Sound Effects

Unrelated to music playback, pressing Select/Play/Pause toggles the Apple TV's sound effects On or Off.

Dolby Digital Out

If you are using the Apple TV's optical output, press Select/Play/Pause to toggle the Dolby Digital's 5.1-channel surround sound On or Off. (This has no effect if you're using analog audio cables.)

AirTunes

AirTunes, added to the Apple TV's version 2.0 software update, enables you to stream music playing from iTunes. This is handy if you want to control playback from your PC instead of directly on the Apple TV. AirTunes also enables you to play streaming Internet radio through the Apple TV (which doesn't support radio streaming by itself), or using Rogue Amoeba's AirFoil software (which enables you to stream audio from RealPlayer and other non-iTunes sources).

Press the Select/Play/Pause button to display the AirTunes screen, where you can toggle the feature On or Off. You can also set up a password (which will be required when connecting from iTunes), or clear it.

AirTunes is also the only way to utilize the radio-like crossfading feature of iTunes (where one song fades out while the next one fades in), which is not a feature in the Apple TV.

tip AirTunes isn't the only way to listen to your favorite Internet radio streams. In iTunes, drag radio stations from the Radio item in the left column (or saved from the Web and stored in your Music library) into a new playlist. Perform a sync with the Apple TV, navigate to that playlist in My Music, and choose one of the stations to start streaming radio.

tip One of the exceedingly cool things about AirTunes support is that you can set the Apple TV to act as just one of many sets of speakers. Imagine you're listening to music on your computer in one room of the house and want to continue listening when you go into the living room (where the Apple TV is located), and then also stay with the music when you go out onto the deck (via a stereo and speakers connected to an AirPort Express unit).

Figure 6.3
Surround sound.

When you have multiple AirTunes-capable devices on the same network, you can stream to as many as you want. In iTunes, choose Multiple Speakers from the Speakers pop-up menu at the lower-right corner of the window, then enable the AirTunes clients (**Figure 6.3**).

tip Airfoil 3, from Rogue Amoeba (www.rogueamoeba.com) extends AirTunes by letting you stream audio from any application, not just iTunes.

Set Up iTunes Playlists

Being able to scroll through your music library is handy enough, but there's a better way to choose music. One of the most powerful features in iTunes is the capability to create playlists that contain music of your choosing. This approach also helps when your music library won't fit on the Apple TV's hard disk.

Playlists come in two flavors: a regular playlist that is essentially a container for the songs you drag into it, and a Smart Playlist that gets populated automatically according to criteria that you establish. Your playlists transfer to the Apple TV during the next sync. (See Chapter 8 for more information.)

Playlist

To create a regular playlist, do the following:

Figure 6.4
Create a playlist.

1. In iTunes on your computer, click the plus-sign (+) button in the lower-left corner of the window (**Figure 6.4**). Or you can also choose File > New Playlist (or press Command-N on the Mac or Ctrl+N under Windows).

2. A new untitled playlist appears in the sidebar. Type a name for it and press Return or Enter (**Figure 6.5**).

Figure 6.5
Name the new untitled playlist.

3. Click the category of media you want to include (such as Music) and select the songs that will go into the playlist.

4. Drag the selected items to the playlist name you created.

Double-click the playlist's icon to open the list in a new window. This can be helpful if you want to see what's in the playlist as you add to it.

If the iTunes Browser is visible, you can drag a genre, artist, or album name to a playlist to add all applicable songs. (Click the eyeball icon in the lower-right corner of the window, choose View > Show Browser, or press Command-B or Ctrl+B to view the Browser.)

Create a playlist based on selection

Another method is to build a playlist based on what you've already selected:

1. Select the items you want in iTunes.

2. Choose File > New Playlist from Selection, or press Command-Shift-N (Mac) or Ctrl+Shift+N (Windows). A new untitled playlist appears in the sidebar.

3. Rename the playlist. Since this is a standard playlist, you can add material to it later by dragging it to the playlist name.

Rearrange items in a playlist

Feel free to drag the items within the playlist to change their playback order. If you have an exercise routine you perform every morning in the living room, for example, you can choose music according to when you're active or cooling off.

It's often helpful to display the list of songs according to criteria such as artist, album, or time: Click the appropriate column header to change the appearance in iTunes. However, keep in mind that this is merely a different way to look at your list and doesn't change the playback order. To view the playback order again, click the first column header (the one above the numbers).

Smart Playlist

Now it's time to get tricky. A Smart Playlist enables you to define a playlist based on criteria that can change dynamically. For example, I tend to listen to a new album multiple times in the first few weeks after I buy it, so I've created a Smart Playlist on my computer that displays items added to the library within the last two weeks.

A Smart Playlist can also automatically exclude items. In a fit of nostalgia one night, I created a Smart Playlist called "Ah, High School," which collects all music in my library dated with the years I roamed the halls of my high school. However, it also grabbed a number of symphonies that were recorded during the same time period. I did listen to classical music back then, but it doesn't invoke the same memories as, say, "Haunted When the Minutes Drag" by Love and Rockets.

So, before I embarrass myself with the other items in that playlist, let's move on to the steps required to create a Smart Playlist.

I mentioned earlier that a Smart Playlist can help if your iTunes library is larger than the Apple TV's hard disk. Let's set up one that transfers 5 gigabytes (GB) of your favorite music by way of example.

Figure 6.6
Create a
Smart Playlist.

1. Hold down the Option (Mac) or Shift (Windows) key and click the plus-sign icon that we used to create a standard playlist. With the modifier held down, the plus turns into a gear icon (**Figure 6.6**).

   You can also choose File > New Smart Playlist, or press Command-Option-N (Mac) or Ctrl+Alt+N (Windows). A new Smart Playlist dialog appears.

2. Under "Match the following rule," choose the criteria that will define your Smart Playlist.

   In this case, choose Rating from the first pop-up menu; choose "is greater than" from the second pop-up menu; and set the number of stars to 3 (**Figure 6.7**). This combination grabs songs that you've rated as 4 or 5 stars.

Figure 6.7
Creating a
Smart Playlist.

Let's assume you don't want classical or jazz music in this Smart Playlist. Click the plus-sign button to the right of the criteria to add another selector to the rule. And in this case choose Genre, "is not," and type "Classical". Repeat those steps to add another selector that excludes the Jazz genre.

note When you add more selectors, the statement at the top of the dialog reads "Match [all] of the following rules," which means every criterion must be met for a song to appear in the list. You can change "all" to "any" if you want to include more songs that might not otherwise be added to the list.

Just below the rules, mark the "Limit to" checkbox, change the number to 5, and choose GB from the first pop-up menu. This option is the key to keeping a lid on the total number of songs that get copied to the Apple TV. Also choose how the 5 GB of material is chosen in the last pop-up menu; this tells iTunes what to include if the rules catch more than 5 GB of qualified songs.

Lastly, enable the "Live updating" checkbox if you want the list to change based on new information—for instance, if you added a new album of high-rated music.

3. Click OK to save the Smart Playlist.

4. Give the playlist a name.

After you sync the Apple TV, the new playlist appears in the Playlists screen (**Figure 6.8**).

Figure 6.8
The playlists you created are available on the Apple TV.

Playlists

5 GB Faves ›
Acquisition ›
Ah, High School ›
Albums ›
AltFolkPopRock ›
Bond-Inspired2 ›
Classical ›
Cocktail Music ›
Cooking Music ›
Date added <1 month ›

note You can include music videos in your playlists, but they won't play along with your music. And remember, multiple music videos can't play in succession.

Editing and deleting playlists

To adjust the settings for a Smart Playlist, select it in the sidebar and choose File > Edit Smart Playlist, or bring up the contextual menu (right-click, or Control-click on a Mac without a two-button mouse) and choose Edit Smart Playlist.

To remove a standard playlist or Smart Playlist, select it in the sidebar and press Delete, or choose Delete from the contextual menu.

tip As you create more playlists, you'll want a better way to organize them other than alphabetically. In iTunes, choose File > New Folder to create an empty folder into which you can drag playlists and Smart Playlists. With the Apple TV version 2.0 software, the folders are replicated once synced, though they look like regular playlists.

tip Want to know the secret weapon of Smart Playlist generation? You can create Smart Playlists that are based on other Smart Playlists. This feature enables you to set up one Smart Playlist containing early 20th century jazz, for example, and then another that includes just instrumental pieces from the former.

Edit Metadata in iTunes

Smart Playlists wouldn't work at all if it weren't for the *metadata* stored with each music and video file. Metadata are supplemental information such as the year a song was released, its place in the order of the album on which it appears, and the composer. When you purchase a track from the iTunes Store, that information is already assigned, but it's not always consistent. That goes double for music you rip from a CD, which gets its metadata from an online service.

More often, I find myself changing the Genre tag so that all albums of one band are on the same page, since genre is a handy criteria for my Smart Playlists. Here's how you can change metadata in iTunes:

1. Select one or more songs to edit. If you select multiple tracks, the changes you make apply to all of them (such as making one edit to all songs on an album).

2. Choose File > Get Info, or press Command-I (Mac) or Ctrl+I (Windows). (That's an "i" by the way.) The Info dialog appears (**FIGURE 6.9**).

Figure 6.9
Getting info on
a single song.

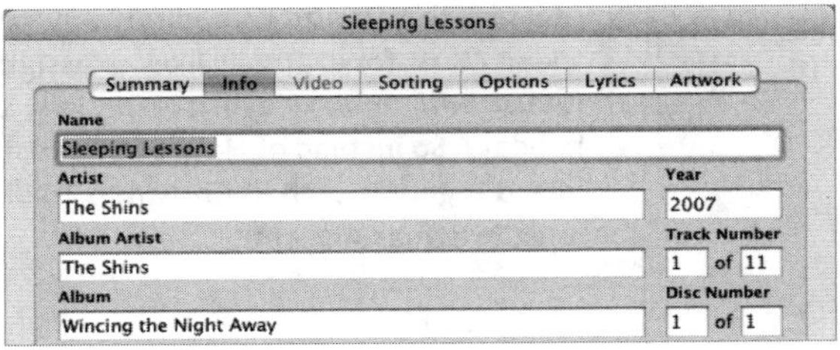

3. Enter or change information in any of the fields. In the case of multiple selections, making a change enables the checkbox beside the field, indicating that the edit applies to all selected items (**Figure 6.10**).

Figure 6.10
Editing data for
multiple songs
at once.

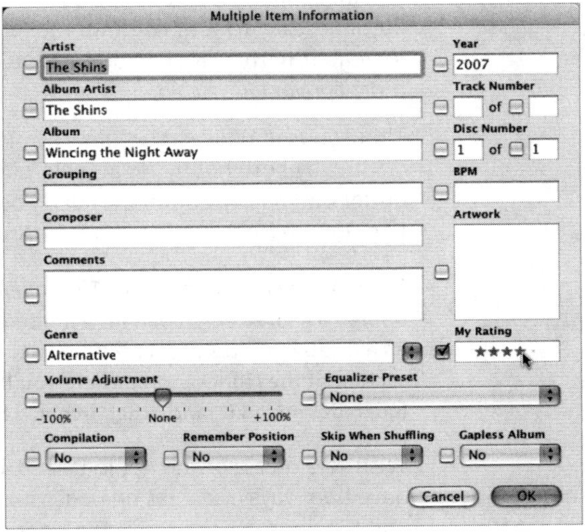

4. Press OK to apply the changes.

Feel free to organize your library any way you wish. My friend Mark, for example, likes to assign custom genres for use with Smart Playlists, especially around the holidays. So instead of Holiday or Christmas, his library includes genres such as Christmas Traditional Choral and Christmas Ancient.

Podcasts

When Steve Jobs announced support for podcasts in iTunes, he described them succinctly as being like "TiVo for radio." Instead of tuning in to a radio program at a certain time of day on a specific channel, the most recent episode is downloaded automatically to your computer for you to listen to (or watch, in the case of video podcasts) when it's most convenient for you.

Thousands of podcasts are now available online, created by both hobbyists and big-name media outlets, and more and more video podcasts are popping up (some of them in HD). And, they're free!

 Some podcasts, such as NPR's *This American Life*, are offered as a free download for a limited time. When its availability is up, it gets shifted to the Audiobooks section of the iTunes Store, where you'll have to pay a fee to download it (and other archived broadcasts).

With version 2.0 of the Apple TV software, you now have two ways of accessing podcasts: subscribing and syncing via iTunes or listening/watching directly from the Apple TV.

Podcasts on the Apple TV

Now elevated to a top-level item in the main menu, you can browse and search for podcasts on the Apple TV as you would for other media in the iTunes Store. To access and play a podcast, do the following:

1. From Podcasts in the main menu, choose Top Podcasts, Genres, or Providers.

2. In the podcast browsing screen, choose a title and press Select/Play/Pause to view it. The most recent podcast is selected at the top, with previous episodes listed below in descending date order. You'll also see info about the podcast episode on the left side of the screen, including whether it's audio or video (**FIGURE 6.11**).

Figure 6.11
Viewing a podcast's episodes.

3. Choose an episode, and press Select/Play/Pause.

4. Choose Play to stream the podcast, or choose Download to transfer it directly to the Apple TV (a good option for listening or viewing later).

If you selected Play, the podcast begins playing automatically using the Apple TV's familiar playback controls. However, because you're streaming from the Internet, you may encounter some rebuffering if you try to skip ahead or back within the episode.

Selecting the Download option sends the podcast file to My Podcasts (found under Podcasts in the Apple TV main menu). You won't be able to watch it until it's finished downloading (you can track its progress in the details at the left after selecting it from the list).

If you stop in the middle of a podcast and come back to it later after clicking elsewhere, the podcast resumes playing at the point where it was stopped. Video podcasts downloaded via the Apple TV also follow that behavior. Not so with downloaded audio podcasts—if you stop to watch a TV Show and then return to the podcast, you'll start over from the beginning. Curiously, this isn't the case with podcasts downloaded via iTunes and synced to the Apple TV.

When you're finished with the episode, you can delete it by selecting it from the list, pressing the Next/Fast-Forward button to highlight the trash icon, and then pressing Select/Play/Pause (**FIGURE 6.12**).

Figure 6.12
Deleting a podcast from My Podcasts.

• NPR: Science Friday

• This Week in Photography

Favorites

Unlike in iTunes, you can't subscribe to podcasts on the Apple TV and automatically receive new episodes. Instead, you can save a podcast to a Favorites list (accessible via the Apple TV's main menu), which provides one-stop shopping for your daily fix. When browsing for podcasts, you'll see an Add to Favorites option at the top of each podcast list.

Choosing Favorites from the Podcasts submenu displays the icons of all those titles you've marked as a favorite. Select a podcast to view the episode list on its overview screen (where you can also choose to Remove from Favorites).

Search for podcasts

If a podcast isn't easily found by browsing, you can also choose Search from the Podcast submenu, which offers the by-now-familiar Apple TV alpha-numeric keyboard.

Podcasts from iTunes

The iTunes Store features a podcast directory, and you can also find podcasts on the Web (using a technology called RSS). In iTunes, when you find one you like, you subscribe to it as you would a magazine or a TV Show's Season Pass (covered in Chapter 5). When a new episode is posted, iTunes downloads it to your hard drive and then syncs it to the Apple TV.

From the iTunes Store

Follow these steps to locate and subscribe to a podcast from within the iTunes Store:

Figure 6.13
The Podcasts category.

1. In iTunes, click the Podcasts icon in the sidebar (**Figure 6.13**).

2. In the lower-right corner of the window, click the Podcast Directory link, which brings up Apple's storefront for podcasts.

3. Find a podcast that interests you. Double-clicking an episode plays the entire episode.

4. Click the Subscribe button to add the podcast to your list of subscriptions (**Figure 6.14**). iTunes asks you to confirm that you want to subscribe and then downloads the most recent episode.

Figure 6.14
Podcast Subscribe button.

When the next episode appears, it is automatically downloaded.

From an RSS link

The iTunes approach to subscribing to podcasts is really just a nice front end for what's really happening. The magic technology behind podcasting is RSS, or Really Simple Syndication, a protocol also used for delivering news headlines in your Web browser or in a dedicated RSS reader application.

Not all podcasts are listed in the iTunes Store directory—you may find a podcast on the Web that lists its RSS feed. If that's the case, follow these steps:

1. Locate the podcast's RSS link, which often appears as an image that says "Podcast RSS" or is presented as a more direct link.

2. Copy the link: Depending on your Web browser, you should be able to right-click (or Control-click on a Mac with a one-button mouse) the link and choose Copy Link Location (or similar).

3. In iTunes, choose Advanced > Subscribe to Podcast, which brings up a dialog.

4. Paste the RSS link into the URL field (**Figure 6.15**): choose Edit > Paste or press Command-V (Mac) or Ctrl+V (Windows).

Figure 6.15
Paste a podcast's RSS feed into iTunes.

Subscribe to Podcast

URL:

http://www.coffeegeek.com/podcasts/
cgpodcast.xml

Cancel   OK

tip

In your Podcasts list in iTunes, some older episodes appear in gray to indicate they're available but not downloaded. Click the "i" icon to view more information about an episode. To grab one, click its Get button (**Figure 6.16**).

Figure 6.16
Getting an
earlier episode.

●	☑ **The Raveonettes – Aly, Wal...**	4:58
	☑ **Devotchka – Transliterator**	4:32
	☐ These New Puritans ... **GET**	11:42
	☐ We Barbarians – Yes... **GET**	3:15

Unsubscribe from a podcast

If you no longer wish to receive new episodes of a podcast, select it in the Podcasts list and press the Unsubscribe button at the bottom of iTunes. Any previously downloaded episodes remain on your hard drive, however. To get rid of them, select the name of the podcast and press the Delete button.

Podcast settings

Subscribing to many podcasts, especially video podcasts, can quickly fill up your hard disk. Plus, once you've listened to an episode, you may not want to keep it forever. The Podcasts settings in iTunes control how the application manages podcasts. To set these options, do the following:

1. On the Podcasts screen in iTunes, click the Settings button. You can also choose iTunes > Preferences on a Mac or choose Edit > Preferences under Windows. Then, click the Podcasts icon or tab in the dialog that appears (**Figure 6.17**).

Figure 6.17
The Podcasts
settings.

2. From the first pop-up menu, choose how often iTunes should automatically check for new episodes: every hour, every day, every week, or manually (in which case you must click the Refresh button in the Podcasts screen).

   The second pop-up menu determines the action to be taken on new episodes: download all, download the most recent, or do nothing.

   Lastly, the third pop-up menu specifies how many episodes to keep before automatically deleting them to make room for more.

3. Press OK when you're done.

 See Chapter 8 for information on controlling which podcasts get synced to the Apple TV.

 Unlike podcasts that you download through the Apple TV, you can only delete podcasts downloaded through iTunes in iTunes—which then deletes them from the Apple TV on your next sync.

Audiobooks

An audiobook is basically a music file, but with the capability to save a paused location—a bookmark—so you don't have to search for where you left off the last time you listened. When you sync the Apple TV, this information is transferred to the computer and also to any iPods that may sync with the computer. The audiobooks sold through the iTunes Store include this capability.

To listen to your audiobooks, go to the My Music submenu and choose Audiobooks. The books are listed according to author (**Figure 6.18**).

Figure 6.18
Let the Apple TV do some of your reading for you.

note If you've chosen not to sync your entire iTunes library, you'll find there's no option for syncing individual audiobooks. The workaround here is to place audiobook files in a playlist and select it to be synced. Confusingly, when you access that playlist on the Apple TV, it will show up as empty. But never fear—you'll find those files in the Audiobooks section of My Music. (Again, see Chapter 8 for more on syncing.)

7

View Photo
Slideshows

Let us ponder once again the words *widescreen television*. The Apple TV lets you watch movies and TV shows stored on your computer, but what else is on your hard disk that can be viewed on a widescreen TV? Maybe the 3,000 digital photos that document every last detail of your most recent vacation, the pictures of your kids at Halloween, and other events?

Add the ability to view online photos via .Mac Web Galleries and Flickr, and you'll soon realize the old days of setting up the circular slide projector are over, replaced by glorious HD video that can display your photos at high resolution.

Sync and Stream Photos

Photos is the only category on the Apple TV that doesn't get its content directly from iTunes; instead, iTunes acts as a middleman, grabbing images from another program or a folder on disk and passing them along to the Apple TV.

As with other media, photos can either be synced to one computer, which copies the images to the Apple TV's hard disk, or streamed from another computer on the network. (The 1.0 version of the software could only sync, not stream, photos.) Even so, making it work requires manual intervention: After you've set up a sync relationship with a computer, the Photos option isn't enabled by default.

Photo sources

On the Mac, iTunes recognizes iPhoto 4.0.3 or later and any version of Aperture. Under Windows, iTunes can retrieve photos from Adobe Photoshop Album or Adobe Photoshop Elements.

 To choose collections (also called albums) under Windows, you need to be running Photoshop Album 2.0 or later, or Photoshop Elements 3.0 or later. Earlier versions will synchronize all photos in the programs' libraries.

On either platform, you can also point iTunes to a folder on the hard disk containing images.

Sync photos to the Apple TV

Once the Apple TV is synced with a computer, follow these steps to enable the Photos feature.

1. In iTunes, select the Apple TV in the Devices list. The Apple TV sync preferences are displayed.

2. Click the Photos tab (**FIGURE 7.1**).

Figure 7.1
The Apple TV's Photos preferences in iTunes.

3. Click the Sync photos from box to enable photo syncing.

4. From that pop-up menu, choose the software you use to manage your photos (**FIGURE 7.2**).

Figure 7.2
Choose a photo source.

You can also use the Pictures (Mac) or My Pictures (Windows) folder as the photo source by selecting it from the pop-up menu. If you want to use a different folder, select Choose folder from the menu and locate it in the dialog that appears.

tip   iTunes recognizes the following image file formats: JPEG, BMP, GIF, TIFF, and PNG. So, any non-photo images (like chat buddy icons) may get caught up in the mix if you specify a folder on disk.

5. With a source selected, choose which photos to sync. By default, all photos are included (the first radio button), but you can also be more particular. Click the [All] events button and choose how many events to include from the pop-up menu; you can select all events or a smaller batch of recent events. Or, click the Selected albums button and then mark which albums to include in the list (**Figure 7.3**). iTunes sees folders within the Pictures or My Pictures folders as albums.

6. Click the Apply button to synchronize the Apple TV and transfer the photos.

Figure 7.3
Enable albums to choose which photos to include.

tip After you've synced photos to the Apple TV, you can use them for the screen saver instead of album art or the floral pictures that are built in. From the main menu, go to Settings and choose Screen Saver. Then, enable the Photos option (see Chapter 3).

Stream photos from another computer

Since digital photos occupy a huge amount of storage space, I can't keep them all on my laptop's hard drive. Instead, they're stored on an external drive connected to an older computer in my house that acts as a media server. Under version 2.0 of the Apple TV software, I can now access those photos without synchronizing them. Here's how:

1. Set up the other computer to act as a streaming source (see "Stream Media from Other Computers" in Chapter 8).

2. In iTunes on the streaming computer, select the Apple TV in the Devices list.

3. Click the Photos tab.

4. Choose source and albums to share (**Figure 7.4**).

Figure 7.4
Sharing photos from iTunes on a streamed computer.

Play a Slideshow

Some devices, such as TiVo units with TiVo Desktop, let you browse the library as if you were on the computer, selecting each image or folder of pictures. The Apple TV takes a more presentation-focused approach, figuring if you want to go to the trouble of selecting each image or navigating a folder structure, you'd probably do it on the computer.

To start a slideshow, do the following:

1. From the Apple TV's main menu, choose Photos in the left pane and My Photos on the right.

   To access photos from a streaming computer, choose the Shared Photos submenu.

2. On the next screen, select Photos to view all photos or the name of an album (**Figure 7.5**). A preview of images appears at left.

3. Press Select/Play/Pause to start the slideshow.

Figure 7.5
Choose
an album.

The Apple TV displays each image for a few seconds, applies a transition, and then displays the next one. While the slideshow is running, you can control playback using the following actions:

- Press the Select/Play/Pause button to pause the show; press it again to resume.

- Press the Previous/Rewind button to go back to the previous photo.

- Press the Next/Fast-forward button to advance to the next photo immediately.

- Press the Menu button to exit the slideshow and return to the Photos screen.

 tip **The Apple TV will not sync with the computer while a slideshow is playing.**

Slideshow settings

In the Photos submenu of the main menu, choose Settings to control how the slideshow plays.

Time Per Slide

Choose this option and then select the amount of time each photo appears onscreen: 2, 3, 5, 10, or 20 seconds. Press Menu to return to Settings screen.

Music

In addition to filling your television with photos, a slideshow can play music from your iTunes library. Choose a playlist on this screen.

tip Set up a playlist in iTunes that matches your photos (see Chapter 6). You don't want to be viewing your Hawaii vacation photos and be interrupted by "Hazy Shade of Winter" by The Bangles or Vanilla Ice's "Ice, Ice, Baby." (Actually, I don't want to know about the latter.)

Repeat

When the last photo is shown, the slideshow starts over from the beginning. Press Select/Play/Pause to toggle this option on and off.

Shuffle Photos

When this option is turned on, pictures are displayed in random order. Press Select/Play/Pause to toggle this option on and off.

Shuffle Music

If you enabled music playback under the Music setting, this option plays songs in random order. Press Select/Play/Pause to toggle the option on and off.

Ken Burns Effect

Ken Burns is a documentary filmmaker who popularized a video technique known as *pan and zoom*, where a still image is shown but the camera moves across it, zooms in or out, or both, to impart a sense of motion. The Ken Burns Effect adds some polish to the slideshow, but it can also cause some unexpected results, such as cutting off the tops of people's heads to accommodate the zoom.

Unlike the effect's implementation in iPhoto or iMovie on the Mac, the Apple TV doesn't let you apply specific start and end states to each photo. (But there is a workaround, which I cover later.) Press Select/Play/Pause to toggle the effect on and off.

Transitions

Choose the Transitions option to view a list of 12 effects to implement when moving from one photo to the next (**FIGURE 7.6**). Highlight the one you want and press Select/Play/Pause to enable it (indicated by a checkmark next to the name). The Random option picks transitions randomly. You can also choose Off, which simply makes images display back to back with no transition.

Figure 7.6
An example of a transition, in this case Mosaic Flip Small.

tip Transitions can be pleasant or distracting. Dissolve, for example, is a subtle and professional effect that fades one image into the next. I also particularly like Fade Through Black, which evokes the sensation of watching a slideshow from an old slide projector. Others, such as

Twirl, seem nifty but can quickly result in nausea. The best advice is to pick a transition that isn't distracting and keeps the focus on the photos.

tip Bonus—but useless—tip! While playing a slideshow, you can press the Select/Play/Pause button to freeze the image in the middle of a transition. I can't think of any good reason to do so, but you can do it.

Create Better Slideshows

The medium may be new—digital photos on a widescreen TV—but slideshows can suffer from the same problems that have existed since the earliest photographers sat their family members down and said, "You want to see all my pictures?" Hours later, glassy-eyed, the family swore never to answer "yes" again.

Don't let this happen to you. Some judicious photo selection will make your slideshows more enjoyable.

Use Smart Photo Albums

Just as iTunes can serve up Smart Playlists, iPhoto and Aperture on the Mac, and Photoshop Elements 6 on the Mac and under Windows, can create Smart Albums that populate automatically, according to criteria you specify. For example, you can create an album that includes only highly rated photos taken during the past month; the content, of course, would change as you add more photos to the library, but you wouldn't need to edit the Smart Album. Or, an album might search the photos' metadata to find a keyword or common term during a set period of time (such as "Emma" between January 1 and March 31). This approach saves you the trouble of scanning your library and locating the images manually.

When you go to the Photos tab of the Apple TV's settings in iTunes, the new album appears in the list of albums to sync.

iPhoto

To create a Smart Album in iPhoto, follow these steps:

1. Choose File > New Smart Album, or hold down the Option key and click the gear button (which is normally a plus-sign button for creating regular albums).

2. In the dialog that appears, type a name for the Smart Album.

3. Set the criteria to define the results using the pop-up menus (**Figure 7.7**).

4. Click OK to create the album. After the next sync, it will appear on the Apple TV's Photos screen.

Figure 7.7
Create a Smart Album in iPhoto.

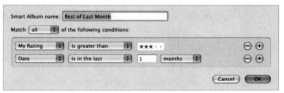

Aperture

Aperture's Smart Albums are created in a similar way to iPhoto's approach:

1. Choose File > New Smart > Album, or click the Smart Album icon in the toolbar.

2. Name the new album that appears in the library.

3. In the attached HUD (heads-up display), enter the search criteria (**Figure 7.8**).

4. Click the HUD's close box to hide it.

Figure 7.8
Create a
Smart Album
in Aperture.

Photoshop Elements

Photoshop Elements 6 added Smart Albums to its capabilities; in earlier versions, you can accomplish roughly the same result by using the Find > By Details (Metadata) command. For this example, I'm setting up the same query as above in the Elements Organizer.

1. In the Albums pane, click the New button (+).

2. From the New drop-down menu, choose New Smart Album.

3. In the dialog that appears, enter a descriptive title in the Name field.

4. In the Search Criteria area, choose an attribute from the first drop-down menu.

5. To add more criteria, click the plus button to the right and specify new attributes (**Figure 7.9**).

Figure 7.9
Creating a
Smart Album
in Photoshop
Elements.

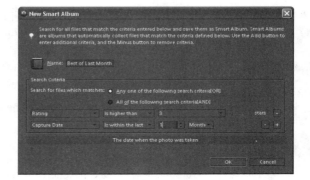

6. By default, the album picks up photos containing *any* of the criteria you specify. To view photos that match every attribute, choose the radio button labeled All of the following search criteria [AND].

7. Click OK to display images that match the criteria.

Create a Custom Slideshow

For more control over how the slideshow plays, you can create one in iPhoto. The Apple TV recognizes iPhoto's transitions, music, and customized Ken

Burns Effect settings. When synchronized, the slide-show appears as another photo album on the Photos screen.

iPhoto

Here's an overview of the steps for creating a slide-show in iPhoto:

1. Choose the photos you wish to include in the slideshow. (This is where a Smart Album would come in handy.)

2. Click the Slideshow button at the bottom of the screen. A new iPhoto slideshow is created.

3. Select a photo in the browser at the top of the screen to edit its settings.

4. Below the photo preview, customize how the photo will appear. Options include applying grayscale or sepia tone; choosing a transition and the speed at which it plays; using the Ken Burns Effect with custom start and end settings; adjusting the time the photo appears; and adding music.

tip iPhoto gets its music from your iTunes playlists, so make sure the same playlist is also synced to the Apple TV in the Music settings (see Chapter 8). If it's not, and the songs aren't available, then the iPhoto-defined music will not play.

5. Make sure the slideshow is selected in the Apple TV's Photos settings in iTunes.

Output as Movie

In other software, such as Photoshop Elements for Windows, there's another way to create a slideshow that plays exactly as you want it to: Output it as a movie. However, since Photoshop Elements outputs movies as .wmv files, you need to convert to a format that Apple TV will accept using the Pro version of QuickTime Player (which costs $30), or a conversion utility such as River Past Video Cleaner ($30, www.riverpast.com) or AVS Video Tools ($40, www.avsmedia.com). For simplicity's sake, here are the steps using QuickTime Player.

1. Create a slideshow in Photoshop Elements using the Slide Show Editor.

2. Click the Output button.

3. Select Save As a File and make sure Movie File (.wmv) is enabled (**Figure 7.10**).

Figure 7.10
Output the slideshow as a movie from Photoshop Elements.

4. Under File Settings, choose a Slide Size of High (800x600).

5. Click OK to give the slideshow a name, and then click Save to output it to disk.

6. In QuickTime Player, choose File > Open File (Ctrl+O) and locate the .wmv file that Elements exported.

7. Choose File > Export (Ctrl+E).

8. In the Export pop-up menu, choose Movie to Apple TV (**Figure 7.11**).

Figure 7.11
QuickTime
Player Pro
includes an
option to export
to the Apple TV.

9. When the export is complete, add the .m4v file to iTunes.

View Online Photos

The Apple TV version 2.0 software fulfilled an item on my Apple TV wishlist: viewing photos uploaded to Flickr and .Mac Web Galleries. I'm now able to check in on the shots my friends are uploading to the Web. It's also a great way to upload photos of the kids so that grandparents and others can view them without doing much more than turning on the television. The initial implementation of this feature has a few frustrations, but it's a welcome start.

Flickr

Although several photo-sharing sites exist on the Web, Flickr (www.flickr.com) is the largest and one of the best.

Add a contact

Before you can view photos from other Flickr users, you'll have to set up a contact:

1. From the Apple TV's main menu, choose Photos in the left pane and then select Flickr from the right.

2. Select Add Flickr Contact and press Select/Play/Pause.

3. On the following screen, enter the name of the Flickr user (taking care to use the same capitalization and spaces), then select Done and press Select/Play/Pause.

tip   The Flickr user name is listed in bold (and in possessive form) at the top of the user's photostream page, which may be different from the name found within the Flickr Web address (**Figure 7.12**). This name is also used as the linked name in your Flickr contacts list.

Figure 7.12
Determining the Flickr user name.

To the Apple TV, my Flickr name is "Jeff Carlson" not "jeffcarlson" (as found in the Web address).

Viewing photos

To view a contact's photos, do the following:

1. Press Select/Play/Pause to view the user's most recent photo uploads as well as all of his or her photo albums (**Figure 7.13**).

Figure 7.13
View your contact's photos and sets.

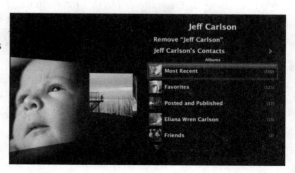

tip On the Flickr Web site, photo albums are referred to as *sets*. Also, you can create *collections* that group together several sets on Flickr. However, those collections won't show up in the Apple TV's album list—just the sets.

2. Choose Most Recent or one of the sets from the list and press Select/Play/Pause to start playing the slideshow (which follows your previously determined settings, including transitions and background music).

3. Press the Menu button to stop the slideshow and return to the Flickr user's page.

tip You'll also see a Favorites option in a contact's list. These are photos the user has found while browsing other Flickrites and bookmarked.

Add your contacts' contacts

Instead of typing the name of every contact you want to add, it's far easier to browse the photos of people your friends have listed as contacts.

1. Choose the user's Contacts and press Select/Play/Pause.

2. Scroll through the list and choose another contact by pressing Select/Play/Pause.

3. On the next screen, choose Add by pressing Select/Play/Pause to include this user in your own contact list.

tip If you first set up your own Flickr account as a contact, you'll be able to use this method to quickly add the rest of your contacts list without having to type them all (slowly) using the Apple Remote.

.Mac Web Gallery

Many of Apple's recent applications, like iPhoto and Aperture, feature the capability to upload content to a .Mac Web Gallery (if you subscribe to the $100-per-year .Mac service). Accessing photos from a .Mac Web Gallery from the Apple TV costs nothing, of course.

Specify a gallery location

To get started, do the following:

1. On the Apple TV's main menu, choose Photos and then choose the .Mac submenu.

2. Press Select/Play/Pause to choose Add .Mac Web Gallery.

3. On the following screen, type the .Mac user name, then choose Done and press Select/Play/Pause.

tip Unlike in Flickr, the name that appears at the end of the Web address is the gallery's name (**Figure 7.14**).

Figure 7.14 Determining the .Mac Web Gallery user name.

On your new contact's screen, you'll see an option for viewing albums as well as removing that user as a contact. Additionally, you can view movies that your contact has uploaded (**Figure 7.15**).

Figure 7.15
View albums and movies from .Mac Web Galleries.

tip   Remember, you can use Flickr contacts or .Mac Web Galleries as your Screen Saver (see Chapter 3).

Lack of Log-in for Online Photos

I'm quite happy to have both Flickr and .Mac Web Galleries join the Apple TV party, with one exception. With Flickr, you might have noticed no steps were listed here to help you log into your account—which means you can't view private photos.

A friend of mine has posted tons of baby pictures on Flickr, which he's marked as viewable only by friends and family. Since I'm identified as a friend on Flickr, I can see them on the Web site, but they're completely missing on the Apple TV.

The same liimitation applies to .Mac Web Galleries, where password-protected albums just don't show up at all. Hopefully, log-in features will appear in a future Apple TV software update.

8

Sync and Stream

Throughout the book so far, I've focused on the most common setup between your computer and the Apple TV: synchronization. After you get everything connected, the standard process is to copy the iTunes library from your computer to the Apple TV's hard disk.

But what if your library takes up more disk space than is available? Or what if you want to avoid hearing Christmas music in June when playing tunes on shuffle mode? Suppose you want to watch a movie that's on another computer in the house? The answers lie in configuring the sync settings in iTunes and choosing sources on the Apple TV itself.

Sync Media Between the Computer and Apple TV

To make things easy, the Apple TV acts as a mirror of your iTunes library. The alternative, *streaming*, transfers media as it's being played without storing a copy of the item on the Apple TV's hard disk. I've covered the initial sync during setup in Chapter 1, so now let's talk about how to fine-tune the sync selections. I'll get to streaming in the latter half of this chapter.

Too much media

When the Apple TV was first released, it came with just a 40 GB hard disk—only half the capacity of the top-of-the-line iPod at the time. After much kvetching from consumers, Apple relented and also offered a 160 GB model. But for some people, that's still not enough (a friend boasts that his music library alone occupies 140 GB).

 Of that hard drive capacity, roughly 7 GB is used by the Apple TV's operating system, leaving about 33 GB or 153 GB of available space for your media.

To compensate for larger media collections, the Apple TV employs a hierarchical cutoff system. Movies are copied first, followed by TV shows, music, and podcasts (photos are disabled initially). When the hard disk fills up, nothing else is copied. However, you can manage the content that gets transferred, as we'll soon see.

tip

If even 160 GB is too restrictive, you have options. Keep in mind the Apple TV is, at heart, a Mac OS X computer that uses standard components. If you're handy with a screwdriver and palette knife (and are willing to void your warranty), you can pull the factory drive and install a replacement 2.5-inch ATA (not SATA) hard drive. For a step-by-step walkthrough of the process (which isn't trivial), see www.macworld.com/article/57079/. Companies such as Weaknees.com can also perform the installation for you for a fee.

If the hard disk is full and you add more content, such as downloading new TV shows, the Apple TV makes room by deleting content at the bottom of the hierarchy.

Authorization

If your computer contains protected content but is not authorized to play it, iTunes displays an error icon next to the Apple TV's name in the Devices list. Click it to see a dialog indicating which items are problematic (**Figure 8.1**). Those are not copied to the Apple TV.

Figure 8.1
Media not authorized warning.

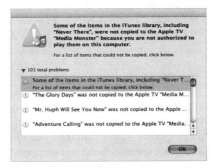

To fix the problem, choose Store > Authorize Computer and enter your Apple ID and password (**Figure 8.2**). At the next sync, your protected content is copied over.

tip Another way to authorize the computer is to simply start playing a protected track in iTunes. The software will ask for your authorization.

Figure 8.2
Enter your Apple ID to play protected tracks.

tip The Apple TV does not count against the five authorizations included with your Apple ID.

Your computer can contain a mix of protected music belonging to different people. My wife and I, for example, store all of our music on a hard drive attached to an older laptop. To make sure the Apple TV plays songs we've both purchased under our own accounts, we simply authorized the computer twice: once with my account info and once with hers.

tip The Apple TV will not sync while you're watching video or photo slideshows for the sake of consistent quality. When you're finished, syncing starts again. However, playing music doesn't interfere with the sync process because it requires much less processor power.

Automatic Sync in iTunes

When the Apple TV is set to sync with your computer, it appears in the iTunes Devices list. Selecting its icon displays the Apple TV's settings (**FIGURE 8.3**).

Figure 8.3
The Apple TV's sync settings in iTunes.

note

The Apple TV item in the Devices list sports a disclosure triangle. Clicking it reveals the categories on the device (Movies, TV Shows, and so on), and selecting those displays the contents saved to the Apple TV's disk. However, you can only see the tracks, not play them. If you're not sure that a piece of media was successfully synced, look for it here.

Choosing Automatic Sync makes things easy by synchronizing your iTunes library using the hierarchical cutoff system. The bar at the bottom provides a graphic representation of the hard disk's contents, while two tabs appear at the top: Movies and Photos.

The Movies tab shows rented movies that have been downloaded via iTunes and are ready to transfer over to the Apple TV (see Chapter 5). The Photos tab remains, as you still have to manually select what photo library to sync.

Custom Sync in iTunes

Activating the Custom Sync option lets you choose what media gets transferred to the Apple TV hard disk. Click the radio button next to Custom Sync, then click the Apply button to switch from Automatic. The tabs at the top grow in number and lead to the individual sync settings for each media type. In each media tab, you can disable the Sync checkbox to turn off syncing for that type entirely.

The Benefits of Custom Sync

Customizing synchronization doesn't mean completely forego-ing the rest of your media collection. You'll still be able to stream what's stored on your PC as long as it's active on the network with iTunes open. When you open My Music or My TV Shows on the Apple TV, you'll see everything that's been transferred to the Apple TV's hard disk as well as what's stored in your iTunes library without any differentiation between the two.

You can even avoid syncing altogether and rely soley on network streaming from one or several PCs (I cover this at the end of the chapter). However, you'll need to transfer some media to the Apple TV in order to watch movies and listen to podcasts when that iTunes library isn't available (i.e., one on a laptop that's left the house). Customizing your sync options gives you that latitude.

tip Clicking the checkbox for Show only the synced items on my Apple TV under Custom Sync takes away the capability to stream media from a synced PC over your network. You'll see only those files you've selected to sync to the Apple TV instead of your entire iTunes library.

Movies

Movies are by far the largest files in your library—a feature film purchased from the iTunes Store weighs in at about 1.3 GB, for example.

When you click the Movies tab, the Apple TV initially limits the sync to the five most recent movies. To change that number, click the first pop-up menu and choose a number from one of two categories: most recent and unwatched (**Figure 8.4**). As newer videos are synchronized or after you watch movies, depending on your setting, they are removed from the list to make room for more.

Figure 8.4
Choose the number of recent or unwatched movies to sync.

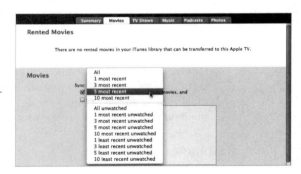

See Chapter 4 for the steps to move rented movies between devices.

Of course, you may have some movies you want to keep on the Apple TV for repeat viewing. That's where the second checkbox and pop-up menu come in. Mark the box and choose specific movies or playlists containing video to keep them on the Apple TV's hard disk.

If you change the settings, click the Apply button to make them stick and sync with the Apple TV.

Just as you can create Smart Playlists of music (see Chapter 6), you can build Smart Playlists that include video. Option-click (Mac) or Shift+click (Windows) the new playlist button at the lower left corner of the iTunes interface and set your criteria. For example, suppose you want to create a playlist containing movies that are between 15 and 30 minutes in duration. Set one selector as Video Kind > is > Movie; then, set another selector as Time > is in the range > 15:00 to 30:00.

TV shows

Similar to the options for movies, the TV Shows settings let you sync recent or unwatched episodes of all your TV shows or selected titles you choose. Or, build playlists that are TV-specific for more control.

Music

In addition to letting you choose between syncing all songs and playlists or just selected playlists, the Music settings tab includes a checkbox to include music videos. If you're tight on disk space and don't watch music videos regularly (especially since the Apple TV limits playback to just one music video at a time), disable this option.

Podcasts

Podcasts operate like TV shows and movies, even though podcasts can be a mixture of audio and video. Choose the number of unplayed or unwatched episodes and which podcasts to keep updated (**Figure 8.5**).

Figure 8.5
The Podcasts sync settings.

As noted in Chapter 5, the blue sphere icon that appears next to an unwatched TV show or podcast episode indicates the file is not only unwatched but hasn't yet been accessed; viewing part of the episode removes the icon, but the Apple TV still considers it unwatched until you reach the end of the program. If you want to restore the icon to remind yourself to watch something from the beginning, it's easy: Select the item in iTunes and bring up the contextual menu (right-click or Ctrl-click on a Mac with a one-button mouse). Then, choose Mark as New to reset its watched state.

Photos

I covered syncing photos in Chapter 7 (since photo syncing is initially turned off). This is where you can choose which photo library to use, such as iPhoto or your My Pictures folder, and select the photo albums to include. Another feature available in the Photos settings tab is the capability to rearrange the list of albums—for example, if you want to put your show-case albums at the top of the list. Click an album name and drag it to a new position in the list, and then release the mouse button.

tip Click the checkbox for Sync photos before other media on the Photos tab to elevate them in the hierarchy, ensuring that photos you've selected for your screen saver won't be deleted to make room for new TV show or movie rental files.

Sync between Apple TV and an iPod

iTunes syncs between your computer and the Apple TV, but it also keeps an eye out for video-capable iPods (or an iPhone), if you own them. As long as your computer is the machine paired with the iPod, iTunes keeps both devices up to date with where you paused in a movie, TV show, podcast, or audiobook.

note This feature applies only to movies purchased to own from the iTunes store and other movie files you've created. As I covered in Chapter 6, iTunes rentals down-loaded via iTunes (not the Apple TV) will start from the beginning after a transfer from one device to another. (Rentals made from the Apple TV can't be synced.)

Let's say you watch half of a movie on your Apple TV but you need to stop and pack for a business trip. To be able to watch the rest of the movie on your iPod while on the plane, do the following:

1. On the Apple TV, press the Menu button to stop playback and go back to the previous screen. (A sync won't occur if video is still playing.)

2. In iTunes, click the Apple TV icon in the Devices list to view the sync settings.

3. Click the Sync button. iTunes synchronizes with the Apple TV.

4. Plug in the iPod or iPhone, which should mount and synchronize automatically. Information about the point at which you stopped playback in the movie is carried over to iTunes and the iPod so you can pick up where you left off (**FIGURE 8.6**).

When you return, the most recent state information (the iPod, in this case) is synced back to the Apple TV.

Figure 8.6
The synced iPod picks up where the Apple TV left off.

APPLE TV

VIDEO
IPOD

Change the sync source

You're not locked into synchronizing with just one computer once you've set up the Apple TV. However, the catch is that you can only sync with *one at a time*. If you want to sync with another computer on the network, do the following:

1. From the Apple TV's main menu, choose Computers from the Settings submenu and press the Select/Play/Pause button. The Computers screen appears, with the name of your current iTunes library listed as the sync source, indicated by a chain link icon (**Figure 8.7**). Choose that library and press Select/Play/Pause.

2. On the next screen, you'll be given the opportunity to cancel or go on with the process. Choose Continue and press Select/Play/Pause.

Figure 8.7
The Computers screen.

3. On the Computers screen that reappears, choose Connect to iTunes.

4. Be aware that specifying a new sync source erases the media on the Apple TV's hard disk. With that in mind, choose Continue on the next screen.

5. Does this look familiar (**Figure 8.8**)?

Figure 8.8
Enter the code on the new computer.

On the new computer you want to sync with, open iTunes and click the Apple TV item in the Devices list, and then enter the code that appears on the Apple TV.

The sync source is changed, and the process of copying media from the new computer to the Apple TV begins.

Sync one computer with multiple Apple TVs

If you own more than one television, you may be tempted to attach a separate Apple TV to each one. The kids can watch their TV shows in one room while you listen to music or catch a movie in another room. Fortunately, each Apple TV doesn't require its own media source—all the Apple TVs can point to one computer's media. Here's how to set them up:

Figure 8.9
Multiple devices.

1. Configure the first Apple TV for syncing, as described in Chapter 1.

2. On the second Apple TV, follow the steps outlined on the previous page to set a new sync source (unless this is the first time you're running the unit, in which case follow the instructions in Chapter 1). The new Apple TV shows up in the Devices list in iTunes next to its housemate and starts to synchronize your media (**Figure 8.9**).

3. Repeat the steps above for other Apple TVs you own.

 tip   You can sync up to five Apple TVs with one computer.

Remove a synced Apple TV

To break the connection between the computer and one of the Apple TVs, you have two options. On the Apple TV, you can specify a new sync source; or, in iTunes, remove the Apple TV from the list of units that the program recognizes:

1. In iTunes, open the program's preferences: On the Mac, choose iTunes > Preferences or press Command-, (comma); under Windows, choose Edit > Preferences (Ctrl+,).

2. Click the Apple TV icon or tab (**Figure 8.10**).

3. Select the Apple TV you want to remove and click the Remove Apple TV button.

4. Click OK to exit the preferences. Syncing is turned off for that Apple TV and its media is erased.

Figure 8.10
Apple TV preferences in iTunes.

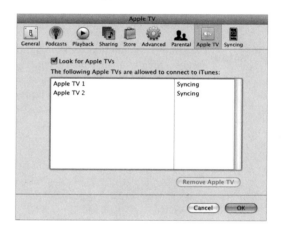

Stream Media from Other Computers

Syncing works really well when you have one Apple TV and one computer, because the Apple TV acts as an extension of your media. And because the content is stored on the Apple TV's hard disk, you can take away the sync source (such as a laptop) and still be able to watch programs on the television.

However, it's increasingly common to find house-holds with more than one computer. As I mentioned earlier, my wife and I have separate laptops and separate accounts with the iTunes Store. Our tastes in movies also sometimes differ. If syncing were the only option, she would have to sync her computer to the Apple TV every time she wanted to watch something from her computer.

note I've also mentioned that we have a third computer that acts as a media server, which is what is normally synced to the Apple TV. However, the same issue remains: If she downloads a TV show on her laptop, she would still need to copy it over to the media server and add it to that computer's iTunes library before she could watch it on the television. That's just too much work.

Instead, she can *stream* the media from her computer. The data is transferred over the network and played as it's received, just as you would watch broadcast television.

tip Actually, some of the media is saved to the Apple TV's hard disk as a buffer to ensure decent playback, but that's just temporary storage.

Streaming is also an easy way to watch someone else's content without a lot of setup. Suppose a friend is visiting from out of town and he has a movie on his laptop you both want to watch. You can specify his computer (running iTunes) as a streaming source and watch the movie—no copying or disc burning or hassle involved.

note Here's the rental caveat again: this rule only applies to movies purchased to own from the iTunes Store and other user-created movies. Rentals must be moved between devices, which requires authorization from the iTunes Store.

Set up streaming

Up to five computers can be set up as streaming sources for one Apple TV. (Counting the unit's sync source, that means you can have up to six connected computers.) Here's how to add a machine to the mix:

1. On the Apple TV's main menu, select Settings and choose the Computers submenu.

2. Choose Add Shared iTunes Library and press Select/Play/Pause.

3. On the computer you wish to connect, launch iTunes.

   If the Apple TV does not appear in the Devices list, check that the Look for Apple TVs checkbox is enabled in iTunes's preferences: On the Mac, choose iTunes > Preferences or press Command-, (comma); under Windows, choose Edit > Preferences (Ctrl+,).

   Click the Apple TV icon or tab, enable the setting, then click OK to close Preferences.

4. Select the Apple TV item that appears in the Devices list.

5. Enter the five-digit code displayed on the TV screen. iTunes verifies and establishes the connection with the Apple TV.

That computer is set up to stream and appears on the Apple TV's Sources screen with a large purple streaming icon on the left (**FIGURE 8.11**).

Figure 8.11
The new computer appears as a streaming source.

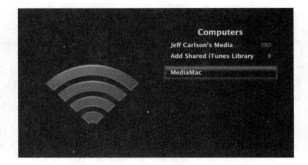

In the original version of the Apple TV software, you could only choose one streaming source at a time. But with the Apple TV's version 2.0 software, any computer that's set up to stream will be included within a new Shared section placed at the bottom of each media type in the main menu (except for YouTube).

For example, choosing Shared TV Shows from the main menu takes you to a screen where your streaming sources are listed, each with an arrow icon (•••>) streaming indicator (**Figure 8.12**). Selecting the source takes you to a screen with the source's name at the top followed by a list of the TV episodes stored in that iTunes library. Choose an episode and press Select to start playing.

 If you're streaming from just one computer, choosing a Shared option takes you directly to the media.

 If you've set up a streaming source, but that computer is either offline or iTunes isn't running, the name of the source will show up in the list but it will be grayed out.

Figure 8.12
Selecting
media from
a streaming
source.

To view photos, however, there's one more step to take.

1. In iTunes on the computer that's selected as a streaming source, click the Apple TV icon in the Devices list.

2. Click the Photos tab and enable the Share photos from checkbox. Then choose a source from the pop-up menu.

3. Click the radio button for All photos and albums, or Selected albums. (If the latter, mark the albums you want to share from the list.)

Unlike the photos from your sync source, these photos are streamed over your network rather than transferred to the Apple TV's hard disk. That's not the only thing that will stream when viewing photos from a streaming source; a random song will play from that selected source's iTunes library when you watch a shared photo slideshow.

Streamed versus synced playback

For the most part, you shouldn't encounter much difference between content viewed from the Apple TV's hard drive and media streamed from another computer. A few situations are worth mentioning, though:

- When watching movies, TV shows, and video podcasts, the video is continuously being copied in the background to provide a playback buffer. If you skip ahead or scan through the video to a section that hasn't yet been copied, you'll experience a brief lag while the Apple TV catches up.

- With music, you shouldn't notice any difference unless your network is particularly slow. Unfortunately, while you can stream music, podcasts, and audiobooks, online radio stations (which stream to your computer from the Internet) are not supported.

 That doesn't mean radio streaming is impossible. See Chapter 6 to learn how to stream radio from a computer to the Apple TV via the AirTunes feature.

- Streaming performance can also depend on the capabilities of the computers serving the media and the speed of your network. This is especially true if one computer is acting as the streaming source for multiple Apple TVs.

Remove a streaming source

To sever the link between the Apple TV and a streaming computer, do the following:

1. On the Apple TV, go to the Computers screen.

2. Choose the streaming source and press Select/Play/Pause.

3. On the next screen, choose Disconnect and press Select/Play/Pause (**Figure 8.13**).

Figure 8.13
Disconnecting a streaming souce.

Connected to iTunes

Your Apple TV is connected to "MediaMac" for streaming. To see its content, choose Shared Movies, Shared TV Shows, Shared Music, Shared Podcasts, or Shared Photos in the main menu.

OK

Disconnect

Alternatively, you can also do it from the streaming source:

1. In iTunes, open the program's preference.

2. Click the Apple TV icon or tab.

3. Select the Apple TV you want to remove and click the Remove Apple TV button.

4. Click OK to exit the preferences.

Use streaming sources only

It's possible to set up all your computers as streaming sources and not have a sync source at all:

1. On the Apple TV, go to the Computers screen.

2. Choose the sync source, indicated by a chain link icon, and press Select/Play/Pause. The Apple TV asks if you want to disconnect from iTunes.

3. Choose Continue. Remember, this step will delete all the content you've already synced.

4. Back on the Computers screen, select Add Shared iTunes Library and continue with the steps for setting up a streaming source listed above.

 To return to a syncing relationship with a computer, select the Connect to iTunes option from the Computers screen and proceed accordingly.

9

Prepare Movies for Apple TV

I'm sure Apple wouldn't mind if you ordered all of your movies and television shows from the iTunes Store, but of course that's not the only source for video. I'm guessing you own a collection of movies on DVD you'd like to watch on the Apple TV, where you only need to highlight a title to play it.

Although Hollywood movies get most of the attention, they're not the only video sources you can watch. If you own a digital camcorder, you probably have a lot of footage already sitting on a hard drive or stored on tape that would be perfect viewing on your widescreen TV. This chapter is all about how to encode that content into an Apple TV-friendly format.

Ripping DVDs

Back in the early days of MP3 music, one of my primary reasons for using digital jukebox software like iTunes was to access my entire library of music from one place, without having to sort through stacks of (admittedly disorganized) CDs to find one album or song. Now, after *ripping* (encoding) my music, all my CDs are in storage and I can find whatever song I want with a few clicks in iTunes.

I'd also like to do the same with DVDs I've purchased.

For example, I loaned disc 1 of the series *Firefly* to a friend and completely forgot about it. Months passed. When I wanted to watch an episode again, I couldn't find the disc. I asked my friend, who said he'd returned the CD shortly after I'd loaned it to him. It turned out the case had slipped behind my entertainment center and was actually within a foot of my DVD player the whole time. If I had ripped the episodes to a hard drive, I could have just pulled up the one I wanted to watch and not thought any more about it.

Here's another good example: If you have children, you know that a DVD takes a lot of abuse until they're unplayable. When it reaches that point, you could explain to Junior that nothing in life is permanent, that all things must come to an end, and that Thomas the Tank Engine isn't the end-all and be-all of existence. But you'd probably end up buying a new copy anyway. With the Apple TV, you can rip that original disc and then put it safely away and play the contents from the Apple TV at any time.

Convert DVD content

Let me say at the outset that video encoding is a topic you could easily lose yourself in. Fortunately, others with that knowledge and expertise have created tools that can convert video to formats the Apple TV can play.

Legal Disclaimer

In case you weren't aware, I'm not a lawyer and I can't give out any legal advice. However, you should know that things aren't cut-and-dried when it comes to encoding some DVD content. (Warning, acronyms ahead.) Most commercial DVDs that contain feature films employ digital rights management (DRM) using CSS (Content Scrambling System) and Macrovision, encryption methods designed to prevent copying the disc's contents. It's currently illegal to circumvent such protections in the United States due to the Digital Millenium Copyright Act (DMCA). However, there's some gray area in terms of fair use, and whether it's legal to make a backup copy of media you own for your own purposes.

If you're at all uncomfortable ripping DVDs, I urge you to skip the instruction in this chapter (at least, the sections pertaining to copying commercial DVDs—no restrictions exist on copying your own video that you've burned to DVD). One of the reasons Apple entered the market for selling movies through iTunes was to provide a way for people to legally obtain digital entertainment, so that avenue is certainly available. And note that I'm talking only about ripping content you legally own, not stuff given to you by a friend or found on the Internet somewhere.

You can find more information at the Electronic Frontier Foundation's Web site (www.eff.org/IP/digitalvideo/).

If you own a Mac, download HandBrake (www.hand-brake.fr), a free, open-source application that can rip commercial DVDs.

note **A Windows version of HandBrake is also available, but as of the publication of this book, I can't recommend it. Primarily this is because it won't decrypt commercial DVDs, making it useless for what we're trying to do here. But it's also pretty rough around the edges, with an interface especially that needs more work. If you're ripping unencrypted DVDs and aren't bothered by interface issues (like status boxes that don't reveal the status), HandBrake for Windows is a good free solution.**

The Netflix Temptation

If you subscribe to a movie rental service such as Netflix, you get to enjoy a steady stream of DVDs delivered to your mailbox. And, lo, you may be sorely tempted. You might be thinking, *Casino Royale* was a good movie, worth watching several times. Maybe I'll just rip the DVD to my computer and watch it whenever I want, and then send the disc back to Netflix.

Don't give in. I'm not trying to be Miss Manners here, but that's just not cool. If a movie is worth keeping, go buy the DVD and rip that to disk.

I have occasionally ripped a Netflix movie to watch on my iPhone or laptop when it's inconvenient to carry the DVD (or when I know my wife is eagerly waiting for the next *Battlestar Galactica* disc, which won't arrive until I send my movie back). But when I'm done watching the movie, I delete the file.

Under Windows, DVD to Apple TV Converter (mp4converter.net) provides the same capabilities in an easy-to-use interface for $30. Several similar utilities are available; I'm using this one as an example.

I'll walk through the steps required to grab the video content and then take a look at some of the specific settings that come into play.

Encode with HandBrake (Mac)

To rip a DVD using HandBrake, do the following:

1. Launch HandBrake. If the DVD isn't in your Mac's optical drive, insert it. HandBrake detects the disc and scans it, specifically looking for a folder called VIDEO_TS.

2. A DVD's structure is made up of titles and chapters. A feature movie, for example, may occupy one title, while a making-of video on the same disc would be another title. In HandBrake, check that the selection in the Title pop-up menu looks like it would be feature length; in **FIGURE 9.1**, title 1's duration is 1 hour and 55 minutes, so that's definitely the movie itself.

Figure 9.1
HandBrake's Title pop-up menu.

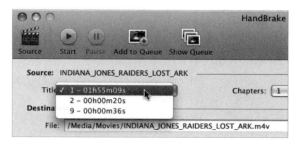

3. If you plan to rip the entire movie, leave the Chapters pop-up menus alone. However, if you want to encode just a portion of the movie, choose the chapter numbers you want; these represent scenes in the movie you can easily skip to when playing the DVD.

 Choose one or two chapters if you want to rip just a sample of the movie to see how it looks when played back on the Apple TV. That way, you won't have to wait for the entire film to be encoded.

4. Click the Toggle Presets button to reveal the Presets drawer and click AppleTV. The output settings are switched to values that generate a movie that will play on the Apple TV (I'll cover these in more detail later).

5. Choose a destination and name for the file that will be created in the Destination field; either type the path name directly or click the Browse button and change the information in the dialog that appears.

6. Click Start to initiate the encoding.

Depending on the length of the movie and the power of your computer, this step could take a while. Video encoding is processor-intensive, so you might want to go grab a cup of tea.

Encode with DVD to Apple TV Converter (Windows)

To rip a DVD using DVD to Apple TV Converter, follow these steps:

1. Launch the program. If the DVD isn't in your computer's optical drive, insert it.

2. Click the Open DVD button and select the DVD in the Browse for Folder dialog.

3. In the list of titles and chapters, mark the checkboxes for the ones you want to encode. All chapters on disc are selected by default, so deselect any that aren't part of the title that contains the movie itself.

tip **Select a chapter in the list to view a preview in the lower-right corner of the application window.**

4. At the bottom of the window, choose AppleTV h264 720P from the Profile pop-up menu (**Figure 9.2**). (If your television doesn't support 720p playback, choose AppleTV h264 480p instead.)

Figure 9.2
Custom profiles available in DVD to Apple TV Converter.

5. In the Profile Settings pane, enter a name in the Name field.

6. Click the Browse button next to the Destination field to choose a location for the generated file.

7. Click the Start Ripping button to initiate encoding.

Add the movie to iTunes

To make the movie appear on the Apple TV, you need to add it to iTunes. Locate the file that the DVD ripping software created and drag it to the iTunes library. Or, choose File > Add to Library (Command-O) on the Mac or File > Add File to Library (Ctrl+O) under Windows and find the file using the Add to Library dialog. The movie appears in your Movies list after the Apple TV is synchronized.

Rip television episodes from DVD

Who would have suspected that people would pay good money for the entire first season of *The Dukes of Hazzard*? Using the steps outlined previously, you can rip discs that contain multiple episodes of a TV show—look for titles with a duration of around 20 or 40 minutes (the actual length of an episode minus commercials).

Instead of ripping each episode individually, Hand-Brake can grab them all at once and save them to separate files. Here's how:

1. Follow the steps outlined in the previous pages to choose a title containing an episode.

2. In the Destination field, give the file a unique name (such as the episode number).

3. Click the Add to Queue button to put that title on the waiting list.

4. Choose another title from the Title menu, give it a unique name, and click Add to Queue again.

Repeat for as many episodes you want to rip from the disc.

tip | Titles can be added to the queue in any order; don't worry about adding them sequentially.

Click the Show Queue button at any time during this process to view a list of what's scheduled to be encoded.

You can click the remove button (the X to the right of an item in the queue) to cancel an item. In fact, if you need to change the settings of an item in the queue, simply remove it and add it again with the new options.

5. Click the Start button to initiate encoding.

6. Add the episode files to iTunes.

Encoding settings, explained

While your video is being ripped, let's go back and look at some of the encoding settings we skipped over in the name of getting speedy results. Tweaking these enables you to massage the output, letting you give up some image quality in favor of creating smaller files on disk, for example.

Here's how Apple lists the supported video formats:

- H.264 and protected H.264 (from iTunes Store): Up to 5 Mbps, Progressive Main Profile (CAVLC) with AAC-LC audio up to 160 Kbps (maximum resolution: 1280 by 720 pixels at 24 fps, 960 by 540 pixels at 30 fps) in .m4v, .mp4, and .mov file formats

- iTunes Store purchased video: 320 by 240 pixels, 640 by 480 pixels, 720 by 480 pixels (anamorphic), or high-definition 720p

- MPEG-4: Up to 3 Mbps, Simple Profile with AAC-LC audio up to 160 Kbps (maximum resolution: 720 by 432 pixels at 30 fps) in .m4v, .mp4, and .mov file formats

Codec

H.264 and MPEG-4 are codecs (a shortened term for *compressor-decompressor*), the mathematical methods of compressing video to manageable sizes. Progressive Main Profile (CAVLC) is a specific encoding method used, essentially a way of ordering the data that makes video delivery efficient. (I could explain more about context-adaptive variable-length coding, but my brain would explode. You can find more information at en.wikipedia.org/wiki/H.264.)

Bitrate

Bitrate is the measure of how much data is transferred per second. The Apple TV can handle video encoded in H.264 at up to 5 megabits per second (Mbps), while MPEG-4 can handle up to 3 Mbps. In general, a higher bitrate produces higher-quality video, because more information is delivered per second. But that also creates larger file sizes. The presets in HandBrake and DVD to Apple TV Converter use 2.5 Mbps (expressed as 2500 kilobits per second, or Kbps) or 3 Mbps as a compromise. Movies purchased from the iTunes Store, by comparison, average about 1.5 Mbps so they will also play on video-enabled iPods and iPhones, which don't have the same robust video-decoding hardware such as is found on the Apple TV or on personal computers. If you're experimenting with the settings yourself, bitrate is a good place to start with other values.

The audio bitrate is also included: AAC-LC audio at up to 160 Kbps refers to audio encoded using the Advanced Audio Coding-Lossy Compression codec.

Resolution

Resolution is the size of the video image in pixels. One of the easiest ways to reduce the size of a movie file is to rip it at a lower resolution (such as 640 by 480 pixels), because you're rendering far fewer pixels. Movies purchased from the iTunes Store are either 320 by 240 pixels (the size offered when video first became available) or 640 by 480 pixels, which can be played on a video-enabled iPod.

Framerate

Framerate is expressed as frames per second (fps). When you have more frames, you're using more data, which is why 720p HD video is limited to 24 fps on the Apple TV. However, 24 fps is also the framerate of projected film, which exhibits a specific "movie quality" appearance. Compare that to NTSC video (the standard in the United States), which runs at 30 fps and has a distinct "video" feel. (The other video standard, PAL, runs at 25 fps and is often used by independent filmmakers to simulate that film look.) If you encode an HD movie at 30 fps, the Apple TV won't play it.

File format

The Apple TV can play files in .m4v, .mp4 (both
MPEG-4), and .mov (QuickTime movie) formats.
What's notable about these requirements is that the
box will not play some other well-known formats
such as DivX or Windows Media (.wmv).

 **Enterprising hackers have come up with ways to modify
the Apple TV so that it will play those and other formats.
See wiki.awkwardtv.org for more information.**

Convert HD Content

Hungry for more HD content (other than the movie
rentals and podcasts that Apple makes available)?
You can also download high-definition movies from
Apple's QuickTime pages and other online sources.
Making them Apple TV-friendly is simple.

Rip Your Own DVDs

I've focused on ripping commercial DVDs because those are usually the discs in your collection you'd most want to watch on the
Apple TV (otherwise, why did you buy them in the first place?).
But these tools work equally well for ripping DVDs you may
have been given or created yourself. The easiest example I can
think of is the wedding DVD. The plastic disc itself isn't going to
last forever (or maybe not even a decade), so you could rip that
video to your hard disk as a backup copy. (It's also something
you can bring up every year on your anniversary without hunt-
ing for the disc.)

If you've upgraded QuickTime Player to QuickTime Pro (which costs $30), simply open the HD movie, choose File > Export, and select Movie to Apple TV as the export format.

Another Mac solution is VisualHub from Tech-spansion ($23, www.techspansion.com/visualhub/), which not only converts videos much faster than QuickTime's poky pace, but also handles some video formats that QuickTime can't read. Apple TV Video Converter ($29, www.mp4converter.net) handles the same tasks on the Windows side.

If the HD source video is larger than the Apple TV's maximum resolution, use the programs' advanced settings to specify a size of 1280 by 720 pixels, set the encoding type to H.264, and be sure to set the framerate as 24 fps.

tip "If I can specify an HD resolution, why not just convert my DVD movies to 1280 by 720?" you may be asking yourself. Unfortunately, resolution doesn't work that way. If your original resolution is lower than what you're trying to achieve (which is the case with DVD), upsampling in this way only adds pixels and often degrades image quality—the computer is guessing where to insert pixels where they didn't exist before.

Convert Your Own Movies

Most digital camcorders include a cable that lets you plug the device directly into your television to play back the video you shot, which is a better viewing experience than crowding around the camcorder's two-inch screen. But that puts you back behind the TV, messing with cables video inputs and audio sources.

Plus, you may have already edited your footage. When friends and relatives come to visit, show off your handiwork (and your vacation highlights) on the television. As high-definition camcorders start to trickle into people's hands, this option is going to become more popular.

Export the video

For the sake of example, I'm going to assume you've already edited your video using a program like Apple's iMovie '08 (free on new Macs, or part of the $80 iLife suite) or Microsoft's Windows MovieMaker, which comes with Windows XP Service Pack 2 (SP2) and Windows Vista.

iMovie '08

If your movie was edited in iMovie '08, do the following:

1. Open your edited movie in iMovie.

2. Choose Share > iTunes, which brings up a share dialog (**Figure 9.3**).

Figure 9.3
iMovie '08's
Share dialog.

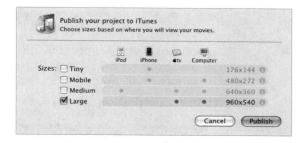

3. Choose a size to export; the Medium and Large sizes are readable on the Apple TV.

4. Click Publish to export the movie. The software saves a version that's appropriate for the source material—HD movies are exported at the Apple TV's HD resolution, for example—and the video is added to iTunes.

tip

If you own a Mac and want to know more about editing in iMovie (and creating DVDs using iDVD), allow me to humbly suggest my book *iMovie '08 & iDVD '08: Visual QuickStart Guide*. It covers everything from shooting footage to burning the final movie on DVD. See www. jeffcarlson.com/imovie/ for more information.

Windows Movie Maker

Follow these steps to export a movie from Windows Movie Maker:

1. Open your edited movie in Windows Movie Maker.

2. In the Tasks pane, click Finish Movie and then choose Save to my computer. The Save Movie Wizard appears.

3. Give the movie a file name and choose a location on disk where it will be saved.

4. On the next screen, click the Other settings radio button and choose High quality video (NTSC) (**Figure 9.4**).

5. Click the Next button to export the movie.

Figure 9.4
The Save
Movie Wizard
in Windows
Movie Maker.

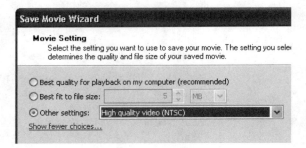

Save Movie Wizard

Movie Setting
Select the setting you want to use to save your movie. The setting you selec determines the quality and file size of your saved movie.

○ Best quality for playback on my computer (recommended)
○ Best fit to file size: 5 ⌄ MB ⌄
⦿ Other settings: High quality video (NTSC)   ⌄
Show fewer choices...

6. Launch your favorite video conversion software; for this example, I'm using Apple TV Video Converter. The steps in most programs should be similar, however.

7. Click the Add button and locate your exported movie.

8. Click the Encode button to convert the file.

9. Add the new movie file to iTunes for later synchronizing to the Apple TV.

Add Metadata

A downside to ripping your own DVDs or converting your movies is that they don't include the type of metadata that make Smart Playlists so helpful. Just a few minutes of work, however, can remedy that:

1. In iTunes, select the movie and choose File > Get Info.

2. Click the Info icon or tab.

3. Enter whatever data you want into the fields provided.

   Since iTunes began its life as a music player, the fields on the Info tab are really music-centric. However, what's important is that you're adding information that can be found later. So, for example, you could insert the director's name in the Artist field and list the major cast members in the Comments field (**Figure 9.5**).

Figure 9.5
Editing
metadata
in iTunes.

tip   To be more specific in your metadata tagging, download Lostify for Mac (lowellstewart.com/lostify/) or one of the AtomicParsley utilities for Windows (atomicparsley. sourceforge.net), which can set tags such as rating (TV or MPAA) and production number that are not editable within iTunes.

Set a preview icon

When iTunes imports a video, it creates an icon based on the movie file's first frame. To give your movie a better appearance, do the following:

1. In iTunes, bring up the contextual menu (right-click or Ctrl-click on a Mac with a single-button mouse) and choose either Show in Finder (Mac) or Show in Windows Explorer.

2. Open the file in QuickTime Player Pro.

3. Drag the scrubber bar below the movie to the frame you'd like to use as the icon.

4. Choose Edit > Copy.

5. In iTunes, choose File > Get Info and click the Artwork tab.

6. Select the artwork that's currently there (if any) and click the Delete button.

7. Choose Edit > Paste to insert the image, which will be used as the icon in iTunes and on the Apple TV (**Figure 9.6**).

tip

You can also create artwork in another application such as Adobe Photoshop. Instead of copying and pasting, click the Add button in the Get Info dialog and choose your artwork.

Figure 9.6
Choose your own movie icon artwork.

Troubleshooting

The Apple TV is designed to be an appliance, sitting next to your television and serving media. However, under the beautiful interface it's also a full-fledged computer. And although the underlying Mac OS X is a very stable operating system, it's not immune to glitches.

This chapter is meant as a springboard for further troubleshooting in the event that something goes awry with your Apple TV. If you don't find an answer in these pages, go to Apple's Apple TV support site at www.apple.com/support/appletv/, which contains the most recent issues and answers.

First Steps

Let's get the obvious out of the way—the things we often skip because they're too basic.

- Check all your cables and connections to make sure they're seated tightly on the Apple TV, the television, and your stereo (if one is hooked up).

- Make sure the television is turned on and that it's set to the correct input. Often this is just a matter of pressing a Video/TV button on the remote several times until you see the Apple TV's screen.

- Make sure you're running the latest version of iTunes as well as the Apple TV's software. Select Settings > General in the main menu, then choose Update Software to search for updates. For iTunes, choose Check for Updates from the iTunes menu (Mac) or the Help menu (Windows).

Network Issues

If a synced Apple TV isn't showing up in iTunes or you can't view media sources from the Apple TV, check to make sure you're connected to the network. From the main screen, choose Settings and then General. Next, choose About from the menu. At the bottom of the screen, look to see if the Apple TV has an IP address.

If not, and you're using a wireless connection, make sure your network is listed next to Wireless Network and the Signal Strength indicator displays two or more bars (**Figure 10.1**). Go back to the Network settings screen and reconfigure the connection, or move the Apple TV so that its signal isn't blocked.

For wired connections, try replacing the Ethernet cable. If it runs to a router or network switch, plug it into a different port.

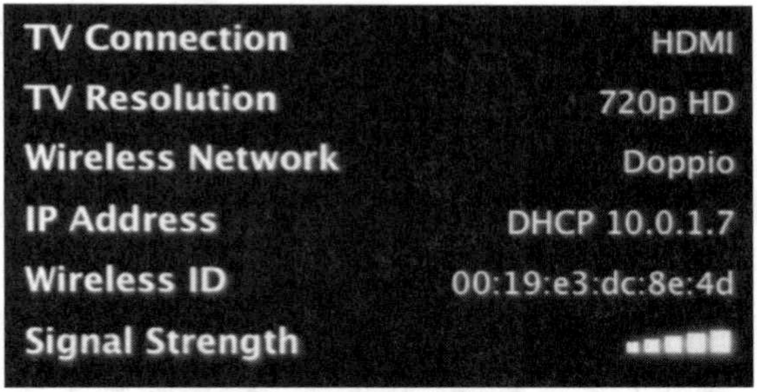

Figure 10.1
Wireless network signal strength as shown on the About screen.

TV Connection	HDMI
TV Resolution	720p HD
Wireless Network	Doppio
IP Address	DHCP 10.0.1.7
Wireless ID	00:19:e3:dc:8e:4d
Signal Strength	▪▪■■■

Apple Remote Not Working

A lack of response may have nothing to do with the Apple TV and everything to do with the Apple Remote. Most likely, the battery is dead (after those long movie-watching weekends). Using a small screwdriver or other object—a headphone plug works nicely—push the small round button at the bottom of the remote to release the battery mount. Buy a new CR2032 coin battery and put it into the mount, then push it back into the remote.

A quick way to check to see if the remote is working is to point it at a digital camera or camcorder (such as the iSight built in to recent Macs); the sensor picks up the infrared light and makes it visible.

Restart the Apple TV

If the Apple TV still doesn't appear to be behaving as you'd expect, try restarting the unit:

1. Press and hold the Menu and Menu down/scroll (–) buttons for several seconds to put the Apple TV into recovery mode. The light on the front of the device turns amber, the screen goes blank, and after a minute or so you'll see the language selection screen.

2. Choose your language, then choose your TV's resolution (if it's not automatically selected). The Apple TV Recovery screen appears (**FIGURE 10.2**).

Figure 10.2
Apple TV
Recovery.

3. Select Restart to reboot the machine from the beginning; this will not erase your media or settings. After a short wait, you should see the opening animation and then the main navigation screen.

Enter Diagnostic Mode

If restarting the Apple TV doesn't solve the issue, try putting it into diagnostic mode:

1. Press and hold the Menu and Menu down/ scroll (–) buttons for several seconds to put the Apple TV into recovery mode.

2. Choose your language, then choose your TV's resolution (if needed).

3. On the Apple TV Recovery screen, choose Run Diagnostics.

The Apple TV reads "Running Diagnostics" while it works. If an error message appears when the check is finished, you need to contact Apple or your local Mac dealer to send the Apple TV in for repair.

If everything checks out, you'll receive a message that the Apple TV is working properly. Choose Done to go back to the Apple TV Recovery screen.

4. Choose Restart to start up the machine again and go back to the main screen.

Restore Factory Settings

If nothing else seems to be working, try restoring the Apple TV to the state it was in when you pulled it out of the box:

1. Press and hold the Menu and Menu down/ scroll (–) buttons for several seconds to put the Apple TV into recovery mode.

2. Choose your language, and optionally choose your TV's resolution.

3. On the Apple TV Recovery screen, choose Factory Restore.

4. Factory Restore erases all of your network settings and media. If you're sure you want to do that, choose Restore on the screen that appears (**Figure 10.3**). Otherwise, press Cancel to go back to the Apple TV Recovery screen.

Figure 10.3
The Apple TV gives you one last chance to reconsider before erasing everything.

Apple TV Recovery

Are you sure you want to restore your Apple TV? This will delete your synced content and you will need to set up your Apple TV again.

Cancel
Restore

5. When the Apple TV restarts, configure it according to the directions in Chapter 1.

note

If you purchased your Apple TV before February 2008, the Factory Restore will set you back to software version 1.0 or 1.1 and you'll have to do the Update Software dance once again to upgrade to version 2.0.

Index

+/- (Menu up/Menu down),
buttons, 7, 25, 26
> (greater-than symbol), 26, 27, 54
802.11 IEEE standards, 12

A

About screen, 30–32, 173
accounts
lack of Flickr log-in, 127
logging into YouTube, 71–72
setting up iTunes, 43
Airfoil 3, 89
AirPort Express, xv
AirPort Extreme Base Station, 11, 12
AirTunes, 88–89, 148
albums. *See* music album; photo
albums; Smart Albums
Albums option (Screen Saver
screen), 34
analog audio cable, 5
Aperture Smart Albums, 118
Apple ID
authorizing computer
with, 46, 132
entering, 43
Apple Remote, 24–29
about, 24
changing reviewing
speeds on, 65
identifying multiple, 26
illustrated, 25, 35
infrared overlap with, 27–28
lining up infrared light
with Apple TV, 27
pairing, 27–28
replacing lost, 29
returning to previous screen, 26
troubleshooting, 173

unpairing, 28–29
using, 25–26
Apple TV. *See also* syncing
adding streaming source for,
145
AirPort Express and, xv
analog audio setup for, 5
basic troubleshooting steps, 172
browsing iTunes Store from, 50
choosing language for, 7, 31
compatible DVD
formats, 159–160, 162
connecting, 2–5
converting HD content
for, 162–163
deleting TV episodes before
syncing, 68
drive capacity for
syncing, 130–131
equipment needed for, xvi–xvii
Ethernet networks with, 10, 12–14
features of, xiv–xv
first syncing for, 20–22
interface of, 23–29
Internet connections with, 18
iTunes authorization
and, 46, 131–132
moving rentals between
computers and, 144
network connections for, 12–16
optical audio cable option for, 5
parental controls for, 78
playing slideshows, 112–116
podcasts on, 99–101
powering on, 2, 6–8
removing synced, 142–143
replacing hard drive in, 131
restarting, 174

Apple TV, *continued*
  restoring factory
      settings, 32, 76, 175–176
  running in diagnostic mode, 175
  Season and Multi-Passes
      unavailable on, 54
  selecting sound effects from, 88
  standby mode for, 8
  status light for remote with, 28
  streaming music with
      AirTunes, 88–89, 148
  syncing one computer with
      multiple, 141–142
  system information for, 30
  transferring rentals to, 48–49
  turning off, 2, 8
  updates for, 19–20, 31, 176
  viewing online photos, 123–127
  wireless setup for, 11, 14–16
Apple TV Recovery screen, 174, 176
Apple TV Update screen, 20
arrow icon, 146
articles in names, 82
artists
  displaying playlist by, 82, 92
  selecting songs organized by, 91
AtomicParsley utilities, 168
audio. *See also* music; podcasts
  audiobooks, 83, 106
  muted during fast forward or
      slow motion play, 66
  podcasts, 98–105
  settings for music, 87–89
audiobooks
  playing, 106
  viewing list of, 83
Authorize Computer dialog
    (iTunes), 132
authorizing computers, 46, 131–132

B

base station passwords, 15
battery for Apple Remote, 173

bitrate, 160–161
Browse link, 39
browsing
  iTunes Store, 39–40, 50
  for media, 50
  My Movies screen, 60–61
  podcast episodes, 99
  YouTube videos, 72–73
buttons
  iTunes Store, 41
  manipulating scrolling with, 84
  Menu/up or down, 7, 25, 26
  Next/Fast-Forward, 25–27, 65, 86
  pressing Menu button during
      music playback, 85
  Previous/Rewind, 25, 26, 64
  Rewind, 65
  Select/Play/Pause, 8, 25, 26, 63,
      85, 87
buying media. *See also* renting
    media
  music, 55
  Season and Multi-Passes, 44–46,
      54, 69
  selecting and purchasing TV
      episodes, 53–54
  steps for, 42–44

C

cables
  analog audio, 5
  component video, 4–5
  composite video, 4
  Ethernet, 10
  HDMI, 2–3
  HDMI-to-DVI, 4
  optical audio, 5
  power, 6
  troubleshooting
      connections of, 172
checking for software updates, 31
closed captioning, 36, 70
codecs, 160

collections, 108, 125
component video cables, 4–5
composite video cables, 4
computers
    authorizing, 46, 131–132
    moving rentals between
        Apple TV and, 144
    multiple Apple TVs synced
        to single, 141–142
    N-compatible, 12
    removing synced Apple TV
        connections, 142–143
    rentals deleted during
        backups, 48
    required for Apple TV, xvii
    streaming photos from other, 111
    streaming radio from, 148
    syncing first time with, 20–22
    unpairing Apple Remote from
        Mac, 28–29
    using streaming exclusively, 150
    wireless connections with
        Apple TV, 11, 14–16
Computers screen, 140
Connect to iTunes screen, 21, 141
Connected to iTunes screen, 149
Connection Failed screen, 17, 18
connections
    Apple TV, 2–5
    HDMI cable, 2–4
    setting up Ethernet, 10, 12–14
    setting up wireless, 14–15
contacts
    adding contacts', 125–126
    adding in Flickr, 123
    user name for Flickr, 124
    viewing photos, 124–125
controls. See playing media
copying DVDs. See ripping DVDs
CR2032 coin battery, 173
CSS (Content Scrambling
    System), 153

custom slideshows, 119–122
custom syncing iTunes, 134–138

D
data sources. See sources
Date view, 68–69
deauthorizing computers, 46
deleting
    podcasts, 100, 105
    rentals during backups, 48
    Smart Playlists, 95
    TV episodes before syncing, 68
DHCP (Dynamic Host Control
    Protocol), 13, 16–17
diagnostic mode, 175
digital camcorders, 164–166
Digital Millennium Copyright Act
    (DMCA), 153
digital rights management (DRM)
    system, 3, 153
disclosure triangle (iTunes), 133
Dolby Digital Out, 88
downloading
    free HD podcasts, 66
    free iTunes songs and videos, 42
    HandBrake, 154
    podcasts from iTunes, 101–102
    purchased iTunes items, 44
    trailers, 58–59
    updates, 19–20
    video, 52
    watching media after
        starting, 52, 55, 59
DRM (digital rights management)
    system, 3, 153
DVD to Apple TV Converter, 156–157
DVDs. See also ripping DVDs
    adding metadata to
        ripped, 167–169
    compatible file formats for
        Apple TV, 159–160, 162
    copyright protection of, 153
    encoding content of, 153–158

DVDs, *continued*
    HDCP and, 3
    making copies of own, 162

E

editing
    metadata in iTunes, 96–98
    Smart Playlists, 95
Electronic Frontier Foundation, 153
enabling parental controls, 76
encoding DVD content, 153–158.
        See also ripping DVDs
    about encoding settings, 159–162
    bitrate and, 160–161
    codecs and, 160
    compatible file
            formats, 159–160, 162
    copyright protection and, 153
    with DVD to Apple TV
            Converter, 156–157
    framerate and, 161
    resolution and, 161
    using HandBrake, 155–156
Ethernet cable, 10
Ethernet networks
    about, 10
    advantages of, 13
    setting up connections, 12–14
    wireless vs., 9
exporting movies
    iMovie '08, 164–165
    from Windows Movie
            Maker, 164, 165–166

F

Factory Restore command, 32, 176
FairPlay system, 46
Fast-Forward, 25, 26, 27, 65
Favorites
    saving podcast, 101
    TV episodes as, 54
file formats
    compatible with iTunes, 110
    supported video, 159–160, 162

Flickr
    adding contacts in, 123
    determining user name for, 124
    lack of log-in account in, 127
    selecting as photo source, 35
    sets and collections, 125
forgotten passcodes, 76
framerate, 161
free
    HD videos, 66
    iTunes downloads, 42
    podcasts, 98

G

genres for songs, 83, 91
greater-than symbol (>), 26, 27, 54

H

hacking
    file formats, 162
    into USB port, 8
HandBrake, 154, 155–156
hard drive capacity, 130–131
HDCP (High-bandwidth Digital
        Content Protection), 3
HDMI (High Definition Multimedia
        Interface) connections, 2–4, 5
HDMI Output setting, 36
HDMI-to-DVI cable, 4
HDTV (high-definition television)
    converting HD content, 162–163
    downloading free HD videos, 66
    renting movies for, 50, 52
    required for Apple TV, 16
    video resolutions of, 17, 163
History option (YouTube), 74

I

icons
    arrow, 146
    preview, 168–169
    restoring blue sphere, 137
IEEE wireless network standards, 12
iMovie '08, 164–165

infrared overlap, 27–28
infrared technology
    infrared overlap, 27–28
    lining up remote infrared
        with Apple TV, 27
    unpairing Apple Remote, 28–29
interface, 23–29
    about, 23–24
    About screen, 30–32
    illustrated, 24
    main screen, 24
    scrolling, 83–84
    using Apple Remote with, 24–29
    Video options on Settings
        submenu, 36
Internet
    advantages of connection to, 18
    entering iTunes Store, 38–39
    renting media directly on, 49
IP addresses, 16–18
iPhone, 49, 138–139
iPhoto, 117, 120–121
iPod. See also podcasts
    syncing between Apple TV
        and, 138–139
    transferring rental from
        iTunes to, 49, 63
iTunes. See also iTunes Store
    adding metadata in, 167–168
    adding ripped movie to, 158
    authorizing computers, 46,
        131–132
    automatic syncing with
        Apple TV in, 133–134
    custom syncing, 134–138
    disclosure triangle in, 133
    editing metadata in, 96–98
    options for podcasts, 104–105
    organizing library in, 98
    photo formats compatible
        with, 110
    required for Apple TV, xvii

setting up playlists, 90–92
syncing Apple TV with
    computer, 21–22
syncing music purchase with
    Apple TV, 55
iTunes Store
    adding songs from browser in, 91
    browsing in, 39–40, 50
    changing location of, 31
    downloading podcast
        subscriptions from, 101–102
    downloading purchased
        items, 44
    entering, 38–39
    FairPlay system, 46
    free podcasts on, 98
    illustrated, 39, 40, 41
    Power Search for, 42
    previewing movies in, 59
    renting movies, 47–50
    searching for media
        in, 40–42, 50–51
    Season and Multi-Passes, 44–46,
        54, 69
    setting up an account, 43
    Shopping Cart in, 44
    transferring rental to
        iPhone/iPod, 49

J
jumping between chapters, 64

K
Ken Burns Effect, 114–115

L
legal information, 31
localizing
    iTunes Store location, 31
    language, 7, 31
logging into YouTube, 71–72
Lostify, 168

M

.Mac Web Galleries
    lack of log-in account in, 127
    selecting as photo source, 35
    specifying location of, 126–127
Mac computers
    downloading HandBrake, 154
    editing in iMovie, 165
    encoding DVD content
        for, 155–156
    unpairing Apple Remote
        from, 28–29
Macrovision, 153
main screen, 24
Manage Passes screen (iTunes
        Store), 45
manual IP addresses, 17–18
media, 37–55. *See also* playing
        media; renting media; watch-
        ing media; and specific media
    audiobooks, 83, 106
    availability of HD movies, 50, 52
    buying on iTunes, 42–44
    hard drive capacity for, 130–131
    Internet rental of, 49
    Most Viewed and Top Rated
        YouTube videos, 72
    playing streamed vs. synced, 148
    rating YouTube, 74
    searching iTunes Store
        for, 40–42, 50–51
    setting up streaming, 145–147
    syncing photos before other, 138
    warning for unauthorized, 131–132
Menu button
    displaying dual-pane menu
        with, 26
    going back to previous menu
        with, 26, 85
    pressing during music
        playback, 85
    using +/- buttons with, 7, 25, 26

metadata
    adding to ripped DVDs, 167–169
    editing for Smart Playlists, 96–98
Movie Maker, 164–166
movie trailers, 52–53, 58–59
movies. *See also* playing media;
        renting media; watching media
    adding ripped movie to
        iTunes, 158
    choosing purchased movies to
        watch, 60–61
    closed captioning for, 70
    controls for watching, 63–66
    converting home movies to
        Apple TV, 164–166
    direct rentals on Internet, 49
    downloading, 52
    HD title rentals, 50, 52
    moving rentals between Apple
        TV and computer, 144
    pausing, 22, 63
    piracy protection of, 46
    playing during syncing, 22
    previewing trailers, 52–53, 58–59
    ratings for parental controls, 78
    rental times for, 48, 53
    renting, 47–50, 51–53
    saving slideshow output
        as, 121–122
    searching iTunes Store for, 40–42
    setting up preview icon, 168–169
    supported video file
        formats, 159–160, 162
    syncing, 135–136
    transferring rentals to
        Apple TV, 48–49
Movies submenu, 25
Multi-Passes, 45–46, 54, 69
multiple Apple Remotes, 26
multiple Apple TV devices, 141–142
Multiple Item Information dialog
        (iTunes), 97

music. *See also* playlists
    audio settings for, 87–89
    choosing songs, 80–83
    equalizing volume for, 87–88
    piracy protection for, 46
    playing songs, 84–86
    pressing Menu button during
        playback of, 85
    repeating, 87
    searching iTunes Store for, 40–42
    selecting and purchasing, 55
    selecting by scrolling, 83–84
    selecting slideshow playlist
        for, 113–114
    setting up iTunes playlists, 90–92
    shuffling songs, 80–81, 82, 114
    Smart Playlists for, 92–96
    streaming with
        AirTunes, 88–89, 148
    syncing, 136–137
music albums
    choosing by artist or name, 82
    displaying playlists by, 92
    dragging songs from iTunes
        Browser organized by, 91
    shuffling songs in, 82
music videos, 81
My Movies screen, 60–61
My Music screen, 80, 81
My TV Shows screen, 67

N

names
    articles in music and group, 82
    determining .Mac Web Gallery
        user, 126
navigation
    displaying dual-pane menu, 26
    iTunes Store buttons for, 41
    submenus displayed for, 26–27
Netflix, 154
networks. *See also* Ethernet
    networks; wireless networks

configuring TCP/IP, 16–18
connections required for
    Apple TV, xvii
Ethernet, 10, 12–14
troubleshooting issues
    with, 172–173
using multiple AirTunes-
    capable devices with, 89
viewing status of, 31
wireless, 11–12, 14–16
Next/Fast-Forward button, 25, 26,
    27, 65, 86

O

optical audio cable, 5
organizing
    iTunes library, 98
    Smart Playlists, 95, 96

P

pairing Apple Remotes, 27–28
pan and zoom, 114
parental controls, 75–78
    enabling, 76–77
    ratings available for, 78
    setting permissions for, 77
Parental Controls screen, 77
passcodes, 22, 76
passes, 44–45, 46, 54, 69
passwords
    entering on Wireless Password
        screen, 15–16
    WEP, 15
pausing
    media downloading, 52
    media playback, 63
    podcasts, 100
    slideshow images
        in transition, 116
    song play, 85
permissions for parental
    controls, 77

photo albums. *See also* Smart
    Albums
    accessing on .Mac Web
        Gallery, 126–127
    choosing, 110, 112–113
    Flickr sets and collections, 125
    using Smart Albums for
        slideshows, 116–119
photos
    shuffling slideshow music
        and, 114
    sources for, 108
    streaming, 111, 145–147
    syncing, 109–111, 138
    viewing online, 123–127
Photos option (Screen Saver
    screen), 35
Photos submenu, 113
Photos tab (iTunes), 111
Photoshop Elements
    creating Smart Albums
        in, 118–119
    saving slideshow output as
        movie, 121–122
playing media, 63–66
    fast forward or slow motion
        play, 66
    music, 80–89
    pausing playback, 63
    playing protected tracks in
        iTunes, 132
    scanning forward or
        backward, 65, 67
    skipping in 10-second
        increments, 64–65
    slideshows, 112–116
    streamed vs. synced media, 148
    YouTube videos, 73
playlists
    audiobooks synced from, 106
    music video, 81
    organizing Smart Playlists, 95, 96
    rearranging items in, 92

selecting from My Music
        menu, 81
    selecting slideshow music, 113–114
    setting up iTunes, 90–92
    single-song, 87
    Smart Playlists, 92–96
    syncing custom iPhoto
        slideshows and, 120
podcasts, 98–105
    deleting, 100, 105
    downloading from
        iTunes, 101–102
    free HD, 66
    pausing, 100
    ratings for parental controls, 78
    restoring icon for partially
        watched, 137
    RSS link subscriptions
        for, 101, 103–104
    saving on Favorites list, 101
    searching for, 101
    setting options for, 104–105
    streaming, 99–100
    syncing, 137
Podcasts dialog (iTunes), 105
ports
    HDMI, 3
    USB, 8
power cable, 6
Power Search (iTunes Store), 42
preview icon, 168–169
Preview option (Screen Saver
    screen), 33
previewing
    movie trailers, 52–53, 58–59
    selected TV episodes, 54
Previous/Rewind button, 25, 26,
    64, 86
Progress bar, 59

Q
QuickTime Player Pro, 122, 163

R

radio, 89, 148

ratings for parental controls, 78

remote control. *See* Apple Remote

removing
 streaming source, 149
 synced Apple TV
  connections, 142–143

Rented Movies repository, 62

renting media
 choosing rental in
  Apple TV, 61–62
 directly from Internet, 49
 downloading selections to
  Apple TV, 51–53
 HD movies, 50, 52
 movie transfers to
  iPod/iPhone, 49, 63
 rental times for movies, 48, 53
 rentals deleted during
  backups, 48
 returning rentals, 53
 ripping commercial DVDs, 154
 selecting movies in
  iTunes Store, 47–50
 transferring rented movies to
  Apple TV, 48–49

repeating
 music, 87
 slideshows, 114

replacing
 Apple TV hard drive, 131
 lost Apple Remote, 29

resolution
 defined, 161
 HD, 17, 163
 setting for TV, 36

restarting Apple TV, 174

restoring factory settings
 reverts to earlier update, 20, 176
 steps for, 32, 76, 175–176

returning rentals, 53

rewinding media, 64–65

ripping DVDs, 152–162
 about encoding settings, 159–162
 adding movie to iTunes, 158
 encoding DVD content, 153–158
 inserting metadata
  on DVD, 167–169
 legalities of, 153
 making copies of own DVDs, 162
 reasons for, 152
 ripping TV episodes, 158–159
 setting up preview icon, 168–169

RSS subscriptions, 101, 103–104

running diagnostics, 175

S

Save exported file as dialog
 (QuickTime Player), 122

Save Movie Wizard (Movie
 Maker), 166

saving slideshow as movie, 121–122

scanning music, 65, 67

Screen Saver, 32–35, 127

scrolling, 83–84

Search iTunes Store Movies
 screen, 51

searching
 iTunes Store, 40–42, 50–51
 for podcasts, 101
 YouTube for videos, 74–75

Season Passes, 44–45, 46, 54, 69

Select/Play/Pause button, 8, 25, 26,
 63, 85, 87

sets, 125

Share dialog (iMovie '08), 164–165

Shared TV Shows screen, 147

Shopping Cart in iTunes Store, 44

Show only the synced items on my
 Apple TV checkbox, 135

Show view, 67–68

shuffling
 slideshow photos and music, 114
 songs, 80–81, 82

signing in to iTunes Store, 43

Slideshow option (Screen Saver screen), 35
slideshows, 107–127
    controlling playback of, 113
    customizing in iPhoto, 120–121
    Ken Burns Effect for, 114–115
    playing, 112–116
    repeating, 114
    saving output as movie, 121–122
    setting options for, 113–116
    shuffling photos and music, 114
    sources for photos, 108
    streaming photos from other
        computers, 111
    syncing photos to Apple TV
        for, 109–111
    transitions in, 115–116
    using Smart Albums for, 116–119
slow motion media play, 66
Smart Albums, 116–119
    about, 116–117
    Aperture, 118
    iPhoto, 117
    Photoshop Elements, 118–119
Smart Playlists, 92–96
    building for movies and
        videos, 136
    editing metadata for, 96–98
    editing or deleting, 95
    getting new music easily
        with, 55
    organizing, 95, 96
    setting up, 92–95
songs
    choosing, 80–83
    downloading free iTunes, 42
    dragging songs from iTunes
        Browser, 91
    editing metadata for, 96–98
    finding by genre, 83, 91
    locating by composer in
        iTunes, 83
    playing, 84–86

    selecting, 80–83
    shuffling, 80–81, 82
    using title to select, 82
sorting
    articles in names, 82
    TV episodes in Date view, 69
Sound Check, 87–88
sound effects, 88
sources
    adding Apple TV streaming, 145
    changing for syncing, 140–141
    photos, 35, 108
    removing streaming, 149
    streaming, 147
standby mode for Apple TV, 8
streaming, 143–150
    bypassing Connect to iTunes
        screen when, 21
    movie files from iTunes, 61
    music with AirTunes, 88–89, 148
    photos from other computers, 111
    podcasts, 99–100
    setting up, 145–147
    syncing vs., 130, 143–144, 148
    using Apple TV for, xiv
    using exclusively, 150
Subscribe to Podcast dialog
    (iTunes), 103
syncing
    Apple TV and, xiv
    between Apple TV and
        iPod, 138–139
    audiobooks, 106
    automatically in iTunes, 133–134
    changing source for, 140–141
    custom iPhoto slideshows and
        playlists, 120
    custom iTunes, 134–138
    deleting TV episodes before, 68
    disabled during slideshow
        play, 113
    during media playback, 22, 132
    first, 13, 20–22

hard drive capacity for, 130–131
iTunes music purchase with
      Apple TV, 55
movies, 135–136
music, 136–137
one computer with multiple
      Apple TVs, 141–142
partially viewed TV episodes, 70
photos, 109–111, 138
podcasts, 137
reactivating after streaming
      exclusively, 150
replicating Smart Playlists, 95
streaming vs., 130, 143–144, 148
TV episodes, 136
system information for Apple TV, 30

T
TCP/IP, 16–18
television.
      See HDTV; TV episodes; TVs
testing Apple Remote, 173
third-party remote controls, 29
Time Machine, 48
time per slide option, 113
Timeout option (Screen Saver
      screen), 33
time-shifting, 14–15
title of songs, 82
transferring
      paused rentals, 63
      rentals to iPhone/iPod, 49, 63
      rented movies to Apple TV, 48–49
transitions in slideshows, 115–116
troubleshooting, 171–175
      Apple Remote, 173
      basic steps for, 172
      infrared overlap, 27–28
      network issues, 172–173
      no image on power up, 7
      replacing lost Apple Remote, 29
      restarting Apple TV, 174

restoring factory settings, 32, 76,
      175–176
unauthorized media, 131–132
using diagnostic mode, 175
turning on/off Apple TV, 2, 6–8
TV episodes. *See also* watching
      media
      adding as Favorite, 54
      closed captioning for, 70
      deleting before syncing, 68
      Fast-Forward and Rewind
            for, 66–67
      parental control ratings for, 78
      partially viewed, 70, 137
      passes for buying, 44–46, 54, 69
      previewing selected, 54
      ripping from DVD, 158–159
      searching iTunes Store for, 40–42
      selecting and purchasing, 53–54
      sorting in Date view, 69
      syncing, 136
TVs. *See also* HDTV
      connecting HDMI cable to, 2–3
      high-definition resolution, 17, 163
      letterbox display on
            widescreen, 60
      playing during syncing, 22
      setting resolution for, 36

U
unpairing Apple Remote, 28–29
unsubscribing to podcasts, 104
updates
      checking for, 31
      getting version 2.0, 19–20
      resetting defaults reverts to
            earlier, 20, 176
USB port, 8
Use for Music option (Screen Saver
      screen), 33
user name for Flickr, 124

V

videos. *See* movies; YouTube videos
viewing
    episodes on podcast, 99
    Flickr contact's photos, 124–125
    network status information, 31
    online photos, 123–127
    TV episodes in Show view, 67–68
VisualHub, 163
volume, 87–88

W

watching media, 57–78
    choosing purchased movies to
        watch, 60–61
    closed captioning, 70
    downloading movie
        trailers, 58–59
    fast-forward or rewind, 65, 67
    finding and playing YouTube
        videos, 72–74
    jumping back or ahead, 64
    movie controls, 63–66
    parental controls, 75–78
    pausing playback while, 63
    playing music videos, 81
    skipping in 10-second
        increments, 64–65
    slow motion play when, 66
    syncing during video or photo
        slideshow play, 132
    viewing purchased
        TV episodes, 55, 66–70
    watching previews and down-
        loaded movies, 52–53, 59
    YouTube videos, 71–75

WEP (Wireless Encryption
    Protocol), 15
Windows computers
    encoding DVD content
        for, 156–157
    exporting movies from Movie
        Maker, 164–166
    HandBrake for, 154
wired networks. *See* Ethernet
    networks
Wireless Encryption Protocol
    (WEP), 15
Wireless ID code, 31
wireless networks
    configuring TCP/IP, 16–18
    802.11 IEEE standards, 12
    Ethernet vs., 9
    setting up, 11, 14–16
    switching to Ethernet
        networks, 14
    troubleshooting, 172–173
Wireless Networks screen, 14
Wireless Password screen, 15–16
WPA-Personal protocol, 15

Y

YouTube videos, 71–75. *See also*
    watching media
    finding and playing, 72–74
    logging into account, 71–72
    returning to, 74
    searching for, 74–75
    selecting Most Viewed and
        Top Rated, 72